BACKROADS & BYWAYS OF
PENNSYLVANIA

BACKROADS & BYWAYS OF
PENNSYLVANIA

Drives, Day Trips
& Weekend Excursions

David Langlieb

The Countryman Press
Woodstock, Vermont

We welcome your comments and suggestions.

Please contact

Editor
The Countryman Press
P.O. Box 748
Woodstock, VT 05091

or e-mail countrymanpress@wwnorton.com.

Backroads & Byways of Pennsylvania
ISBN 978-0-88150-903-8

Book design by Hespenheide Design
Map by Erin Greb Cartography, © The Countryman Press
Interior photos by the author unless otherwise specified
Composition by Chelsea Cloeter

Published by The Countryman Press, P.O. Box 748, Woodstock, VT 05091

Distributed by W. W. Norton & Company, Inc., 500 Fifth Avenue, New York, NY 10110

Printed in the United States of America

10 9 8 7 6 5 4 3 2 1

Acknowledgments

Writing a book requires two types of friends—those who help you work on it and those who forgive you for being neglectful and erratic while you're working on it. Oftentimes these are the same people, and I'm fortunate to have them in my life.

Special thanks go to Abbie Lamb Siskin for her help with Erie and environs, Meredith Brett for her input on Bucks County, and Milan Mitra for his assistance with the forest chapters and anthracite country. Blair Thornburgh produced invaluable fieldwork on the Laurel Highlands, greater Johnstown, and around the Juniata. As always, I'm indebted to those who provided encouragement, counsel, and notes along the way, including Zach Blattner, Kate Dempsey, Chris Kingsley, Sarah Lorr, Gary McDonogh, Maura O'Brien, Gabrielle Ohayon, Karen Revere, Mark Robinson, Eric Siskin, Katie Thomas, Nika Trufanova, and many more.

My editors at Countryman Press are always a pleasure to work with. Lisa Sacks was terrific at every step of the process. And Acquisitions Editor Kim Grant deserves a medal for the caring, selfless way she shepherds young writers through the publishing universe (especially those like me who would be completely lost without her).

Last but never least, thanks to my parents, Arlene and Bernard, as well as my talented sister, Madeline. And I owe special gratitude to my grandmother Edith Sensky, who is a phenomenal woman and a constant inspiration. I love you all more than I can say.

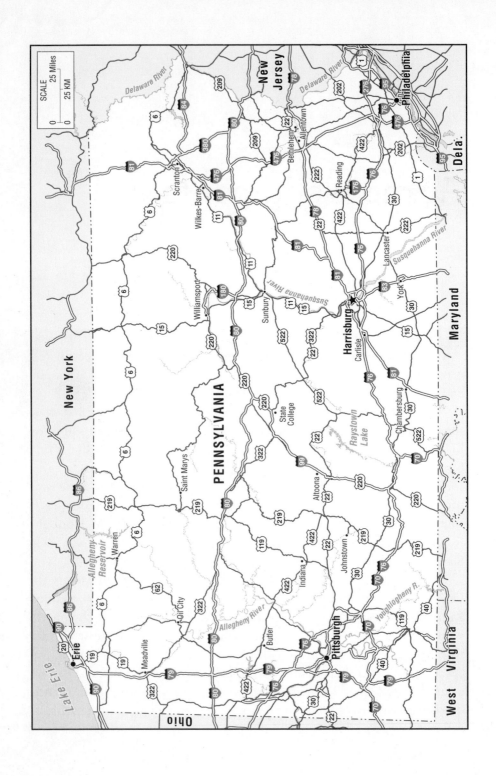

Contents

Introduction

The country itself, its soil, air, water, seasons, and produce,
both natural and artificial, is not to be despised.

—William Penn, describing Pennsylvania in a letter to King Charles II
(*Pennsylvania: Birth of a Nation,* Sylvester K. Stevens)

I had the time of my life researching this book. I hope that comes through in the writing. A travel guide is worth little if the author's observations cannot entice the reader into exploring the subject matter. Fortunately for me, Pennsylvania is easy to love. The state is blessed with 45,000 miles of rivers and streams, nearly 8 million acres of farmland, and thousands of miles of picturesque country roads connecting it all together. From the Endless Mountains in the northeast to the Laurel Highlands in the southwest, no Pennsylvania region wants for scenic vistas and lush plant life. Driving around the commonwealth inevitably brings travelers zigzagging around ridges, over pristine rivers, and through vast hemlock forests. Not that I recommend it, but you can even get a good dose of Pennsylvania green while rolling alongside the semis on I-80.

History
Pennsylvania has resembled its current topography for approximately 400 million years. Prior to this time the islands that became Appalachia experienced periodic erosion on a massive scale. Colossal movements in the region's geography rearranged great stacks of sandstone, forming the ribbon of mountains that stretches across the commonwealth as well as the corresponding river valleys. Ocean water rushed in and out, changing the

landforms as it came and went, leaving intact an ecologically diverse chunk of the North American continent bounded by the Atlantic in the east and Lake Erie in the northwest. This Paleozoic Era spectacle not only formed the eclectic surface geography that makes up Pennsylvania today; it also cultivated an exceptionally useful portfolio of natural resources underground that made the state's industrial age economic boom possible.

Long after the land formations took shape, Lenni-Lenape Indians settled the eastern portion of Pennsylvania—territory they continued to occupy through the early waves of European immigration until reprehensible 18th-century policies forced them west into Ohio. The original European arrivals were Swedes who inhabited land near present-day Philadelphia from 1643 to 1654. The Swedish colony was followed by a tenuous Dutch settlement that gave way to English rule a few years later. King Charles II deeded the colony to William Penn in 1681, and the ambitious Quaker radical went about assembling an exceptionally free society (at least by the standards of the era) around the Delaware Valley.

Penn created three counties—Philadelphia, Bucks, and Chester—in the state's southeast corner, where arable land was plentiful and near the commercially valuable Delaware River. Agriculture dominated from the start, even in Philadelphia, where Penn made his city blocks unusually large to accommodate farming. Corn was a staple crop; cultivation methods were already well established by the Lenape and Swedes who preceded Penn. Increasingly sophisticated farming techniques brought the widespread production of wheat and allowed farmers to expend more time and energy on breeding livestock or developing new trades. Settlements moved north and west steadily, stopping only when they hit the Allegheny Front. Eventually the mountains were conquered and the rest of the state gradually filled out, though the steep northern tier remains sparsely populated to this day. New counties were created when popular sentiment reached a tipping point—farmers who needed to file documents or settle land disputes and tax bills had to travel prohibitively long distances to the county seat and consequently demanded better access to local government. Disagreements often broke out in the state legislature over this (few counties were ready to cede any tax base without a fight), and awkward compromises were struck, sometimes resulting in multiple counties relinquishing land to form a new one. Penn's three counties had become 67 by 1878, and that number has remained the same to the present day.

About This Guide

The rich history of the state's distinct regions and the development of their towns make for great driving tours: surprises and stories lurk around every twist and turn. Chapters are loosely themed in an attempt to provide some coherence and perspective to the state's history and culture. There are deviations from this rule, but for the most part each route is held together by a discrete narrative. But even if nothing of historical consequence ever happened here, the 17 drives in this book would be worth taking for the natural beauty alone.

The first chapter covers Bucks County, one of the three counties settled by William Penn, where the European colonists clashed with the Lenni-Lenape Indians and where Philadelphia's inner-ring suburbs quickly turn to picturesque country towns. Chapter 2 runs through the Pocono Mountains and examines how the region's tourist economy has evolved over the years. Chapter 3 covers anthracite country and Pennsylvania's complicated relationship with the hard coal industry. Chapters 4, 5, 6, and 7 explore different portions of the northern tier timber region, where the logging boom and its subsequent bust have given way to an incredible second-generation regrowth that makes these drives the most consistently scenic in the book. Chapter 8 wraps around the far northwest through the state's wine country and along the Lake Erie beach. Chapter 9 tracks Pennsylvania's unsung history with the oil industry. Chapters 10 and 14 focus on distinctive natural regions in the southern part of the state—the mountainous Laurel Highlands in the southwest and the valley around the Juniata River in the south central. Chapters 11 and 13 return to the state's bread-and-butter industrial pursuits, with tours around the southwest steel region and the railroading juggernaut that took hold nearby. Chapter 12 cuts through the state's center, where quaint college towns enjoy a peaceful country existence within a lush agricultural region. Chapter 15 retraces the state's Civil War history. Chapter 16 peeks into the world of the Amish who continue to thrive throughout Pennsylvania, with a population centered around (though hardly limited to) greater Lancaster. And chapter 17 closes out the book where the American story began, with a tour of southeast Pennsylvania's Revolutionary War sites, from the Paoli Battlefield to the winter camp at Valley Forge.

In a way this was a very difficult book to write, because the sheer number of suitable routes made mapping out a dozen and a half drives a little tricky. My process was guided by two basic rules: to include routes touching every part of the state and to design routes that incorporated the most interesting history, geography, and activities along the way. Certain areas are unfortunately neglected. The big cities—Philadelphia and Pittsburgh—get scant attention, though both have scenic areas within their city limits. They are each located close to multiple drives, however, and some travelers may find it desirable to combine a route or two with an overnight stay in the city. Also missing from the book are some interesting smaller cities like Bethlehem in the Lehigh Valley, the state capital of Harrisburg, and Hershey, none of which could be smoothly integrated into a scenic route. There are also a couple unusual sites I would have liked to include, such as the Jimmy Stewart Museum in Indiana, Pennsylvania (the actor's birthplace), and the Zippo lighter factory in Bradford. These failings aside, I did get to include the vast majority of my favorite places. Drives touch Prince Gallitzin State Park, Presque Isle, River Road, Ricketts Glen, Cook Forest, Straub Brewery, and several minor-league baseball stadiums—merely a sampling of the things I love about my adopted state.

Modern-Day Pennsylvania

While other areas of the country have succumbed to urban sprawl, Pennsylvania still has great small towns. The region's natural beauty surely contributes to this, since even the most ordinary Main Street looks good set against a backdrop of rolling hills, but most of Pennsylvania is inhabited by proud locals who provide essential civic energy and keep their towns humming. The English settled Pennsylvania earlier than many American territories, so civil institutions like colleges and churches had a long time to grow roots throughout the region. Small colleges and universities function as economic anchors, providing a jobs base and year-round economic security to villages that might otherwise rely on a seasonal economy. As a consequence, these small towns have a sufficient number of year-round residents and summer visitors to support family-owned hardware stores, twin-screen cinemas, coffee shops, and diners. Local farms can sell their produce, eggs, and dairy within a close radius, oftentimes neighbor to neighbor.

I don't mean to be Pollyannaish. Undeniably and unfortunately, the slow but steady flight of manufacturing jobs has hit Rust Belt states like Pennsylvania very hard. The boarded-up storefront is a heartbreakingly common sight in many small towns where the local economy failed to diversify after a key industry fled and that lack a more permanent asset like a local college or hospital. And some places have hung on economically but depend exclusively on retirees who love the area and have chosen to stay; if a town's young people are leaving and there's no new investment coming in, it's hard to shake the sense that the best days are in the past. "It's a lovely place," one elderly resident of a charming central Pennsylvania town told me, "but if you're looking for a job, you're out of luck."

Nevertheless, Pennsylvania has made steady progress in meeting these considerable challenges. New investments have stoked the commonwealth's impressive educational and health care infrastructure, while an innate cultural conservatism and environmental consciousness have tempered overdevelopment where it threatens a way of life—one reason the state has avoided the boom and bust cycles now ravaging the Sunbelt. To cite just one example, humble Erie County, in the northwest corner of the state, has enjoyed one of the country's strongest real estate markets over the last few years. Hesitant to change and protective of her natural resources, Pennsylvania is among the most livable, beautiful states in the union. Just see for yourself.

HELPFUL HINTS FOR NAVIGATING PENNSYLVANIA

- Pennsylvania's state roads are sprinkled with speed traps. Watch out for the long, open stretches where speed limits dip suddenly within a mile or two of a town's business district. And if you do get nabbed, don't make the same mistake I made one unfortunate spring morning and reach into a nondescript black bag for my wallet as the state trooper approached the car. They get very jumpy—and rightly so—when you do that.
- The quantity and quality of lodging options varies widely by route. Careful planning is the best way to ensure a good night's rest. Arrange for accommodations ahead of time when possible, particularly in the state's less-populated areas where hotels and motels are few and far between.
- This should go without saying, but since some drives recommend stops at breweries and wineries, make sure to drink responsibly. Do as Lew Bryson advises in *Pennsylvania Breweries* (incidentally, a terrific book) and drink a pint of water for every two pints of beer, not just to stay sober but to cut off all hangovers before they can take root.
- This book is hardly the last word on driving backcountry Pennsylvania. Depending on your interests, tastes, and schedule, you may wish to modify routes, extend them, or incorporate additional sites. The state's Department of Community and Economic Development has put together a well-designed Web site (www.visitpa.com) that assists visitors in crafting their own scenic drives.

Bowman's Hill Wildflower Preserve

Scenic Bucks

Estimated length: 50 miles
Estimated time: 1–2 days

Getting there: This drive runs south to north alongside the Delaware River from Morrisville to Kintnersville and then hooks south to Nockamixon State Park. Follow PA 32 north, also known as River Road, through most of Bucks County. River Road joins PA 611 south in Kintnersville. Take this route for 5 miles, make a right on Durham Road, and then a quick left on PA 563 south into Nockamixon, where the drive concludes.

Highlights: A storied and scenic drive, this route tracks the Delaware Canal from lower Bucks County where William Penn built his Pennsylvania estate to countrified upper Bucks, where the horse farms outnumber the national chain stores. Highlights include Washington Crossing Historic Park, the point from which then-general George Washington led his ragtag Revolutionary Army across the river to a surprise victory over Hessian mercenaries at the Battle of Trenton; the art colony of New Hope; and assorted recreational pastimes at Nockamixon State Park.

Philadelphia is well established as a city of neighborhoods, and its suburbs are similarly distinct. From the mansions of the Main Line to the blue collar hamlets of Delaware County, these southeast communities reveal disparate sides to the suburban experience. Their evolution from virgin wilderness has naturally followed a more leisurely pace than that of Philadelphia, which became a bustling port city from its infancy. But Philadelphia is geographically large and supports several quasi-suburban neighborhoods within its city limits. As a consequence, rural Pennsylvania fans out quickly from the inner suburban core, and development activities are carefully watched—particularly in farming areas throughout upper Bucks County (only an hour's drive from the central city), where this route terminates.

Among Philadelphia's first suburbanites was William Penn himself. During the four years he spent supervising the creation of his colony, Penn inhabited a large estate on the banks of the Delaware River in present-day Bucks. Born into wealth during the first English Civil War, Penn defied his Anglican upbringing and converted to Quakerism as a young adult. This conversion would earn him pariah status throughout his life and lead to multiple prison terms in England. Despite his disagreements with the Anglican elite, he persuaded King Charles II to grant him a large piece of colonial America as a way for the king to make good on a debt owed to his father. Penn used the colony—Pennsylvania, or "Penn's Woods"—to form a society grounded in religious freedom, a conceit motivated by his experiences in Anglican England. It was an ambitious experiment, though Penn governed as an imperfect statesman. He was, for example, an unreformed slaveholder.

When Penn arrived in his colony in 1682, he had a 43-acre estate constructed near **Morrisville,** just across the Delaware River from what is now Trenton, New Jersey. From this perch he oversaw the colony's early development, though he remained preoccupied with his mucky financial affairs in England and spent only four years in Pennsylvania. Penn left Bucks County for good in 1701 and would die 17 years later with his finances and spirit in a shambles. After Penn's death, his sons and associates brought interminable shame on Pennsylvania, cheating the Lenape at every turn and even attempting to break the doctrine of religious tolerance that was a first principle of the colony's founding. But the groundwork Penn laid with his original charter had durable effects on the state. Efforts to deny religious groups sanctuary in Pennsylvania were mostly rebuffed; the lasting settlements of Catholics, Anabaptists, Jews, and other minority groups throughout the state are a testament to that.

Those interested in this history and Penn's story can locate **Pennsbury**

Manor, a re-creation of Penn's home and grounds on the Delaware, rebuilt as part of a Works Progress Administration project in 1939. It's a remarkably earnest attraction—forthright about Penn's ideological inconsistency on the slavery question, and even willing to devote exhibit space to historical analyses that deem the WPA project a "monstrosity." Regrettably, the route to Pennsbury Manor is unscenic. The site is tucked away 8 miles south from downtown Morrisville behind a large industrial park, and the directional signs necessarily lead visitors past a landfill.

This drive opts instead to follow a more picturesque route north, running 40 miles parallel to the Delaware River and then hooking west toward beautiful Nockamixon State Park. The bulk of the route also clings to the Delaware Canal, among the country's great early attempts at large scale infrastructure, built to transport anthracite coal from the state's northeast mountains to Philadelphia in the early 19th century. The canal moved several hundred thousand tons of coal annually during its peak years, helping to power the country's industrial boom and spawning a regional folklore of life along the towpath. Closed to mules and rafts since 1931, the route has been preserved by the state's Department of Conservation and Natural Resources as **Delaware Canal State Park** for the enjoyment of recreationalists. Much has been left intact, including the 23 canal locks. Picnic tables and restroom facilities have been set up at various points along the route, and informational panels add historical context.

Unfortunately, the Delaware is prone to flooding, a reality that has made maintaining the park (not to mention the adjacent riverside residences and businesses) an ongoing challenge. At press time, a four-year restoration project was on the cusp of completion, meaning uninterrupted access along the entire 60-mile towpath. The clay surface is ideal for a hybrid bicycle, though joggers also use the towpath extensively. With several access points off River Road, the trail works just as well for a brief afternoon stroll as it does for a long-distance run.

This drive parallels the middle two thirds of the canal, which in actuality extends north to Easton and south to Bristol. Begin in Morrisville, approximately 10 miles upriver from Bristol. A good starting point is where PA 32 (alternately known as River Road) meets the Calhoun Street Bridge—located just east of the town's diffuse business district. Look over the Delaware into Trenton and observe the capital city skyline crowned by the gold-domed State House. Travel north, resisting the temptation to park somewhere and relax on the benches and docks built along the riverbanks.

Most shore-side land on this portion of the drive is privately owned. Along this segment the towpath and canal lie west of River Road, but they switch positions at intermittent points upriver. When the park lies east of the byway, you'll naturally find greater public access to the Delaware.

Yardley is the next major town, roughly 5 miles from Morrisville. A mill village turned thriving inner-ring suburb, Yardley boasts a chic steakhouse on the west side of River Road and New American cuisine served alfresco at the **Yardley Inn** nearby. The town is also a gateway to the McConkey's Ferry section of **Washington Crossing Historic Park.** Before the canal and the mills brought economic relevance to Bucks County's riverbanks, this area was the site of Washington's historic crossing of the Delaware, a key early turning point of the American Revolution without which the cause could well have been lost. To honor the event, the settlement north of Yardley changed its name from Taylorsville to **Washington Crossing,** a name the town still uses today. Notable sites around here include Crossing Vineyards and Winery, which hosts a popular wine and music summer concert series.

The image of Washington triumphantly crossing the Delaware was immortalized years after the Battle of Trenton in a famous painting by Emanuel Leutze, though as park rangers explain, the crossing's reality was a lot less romantic than the scene suggests. For a slightly more authentic take, visit the park on Christmas, when local volunteers reenact the crossing. They make the trip on historically accurate flat-bottomed boats, which

---

GEORGE WASHINGTON'S CROSSING OF THE DELAWARE

During the dark, freezing December of 1776, George Washington and his Revolutionary Army camped out on the riverbanks north of Yardley. The war had only begun a year and a half prior, but the Continentals had already been routed up and down the East Coast, losing New York City to British forces in September and suffering a naval loss a month later at the Battle of Valcour Island. The Second Continental Congress had fled Philadelphia, fearing continued British victories through the mid-Atlantic region. But on an icy, foggy Christmas Day, Washington ferried his troops across the Delaware River and launched a surprise attack on Hessian mercenaries stationed in New Jersey to win the Battle of Trenton. Over the next week he beat back the British reinforcements sent down from New York, thereby clinching the victory. It marked a turn in momentum that brought the Continental Army back from the brink of defeat and helped legitimize the revolution in the eyes of skeptical colonists and foreign governments.

Fowl congregate on the Delaware River shore in New Hope.

can be seen stored at the Durham Boat House year-round. Like the park visitors center and blacksmith shop, the boathouse is located in the southern (McConkey's Ferry) section of the park. You can also tour McConkey's Ferry Inn down here, a Colonial-era tavern replete with beehive oven and period furniture. Five miles upriver from the McConkey's Ferry is the northern (or Thompson's Mill) section. Take a short but steep side trip up to Bowman's Hill Tower and enjoy the view from 380 feet above sea level. You may also want to stop at the Thompson-Neely House, a handsome stone house that was adapted into a war hospital to treat Continental Army soldiers suffering during their winter encampment at Taylorsville. Finally, for those who can't get enough Revolutionary history, between the two sections of the park is the David Library of the American Revolution, which contains a wealth of rare, primary source documentation on Revolutionary-era history. Though technically on River Road, the library is set back a fair distance, fronted by a swath of farmland.

The best attraction in Washington Crossing Historic Park is **Bowman's Hill Wildflower Preserve,** located in the Thompson's Mill section. Drive up to the motion-detecting front gate and find a hundred acres of native plants and trees scattered throughout a dozen trail sites. Close to half the plant species found in Pennsylvania are growing somewhere in the preserve at some time of year. Meander around the Penn's Woods section and look for old-growth forest, then cross the preserve's stone bridge to explore the azaleas in springtime, the sunflowers in August, and the hundreds of other varieties that bloom throughout the lush free-form gardens. Knowledgeable staffers organize walking tours and direct visitors to areas of interest.

Not far down the road from Washington Crossing is **New Hope**—the famed artists' colony and popular weekend getaway. A onetime cotton and grain mill town that thrived during the canal's heyday, New Hope has enjoyed a second act as a hot spot for painters, writers, composers, and actors from the 1930s onward. Its tranquility and relative accessibility to Manhattan were main reasons why; well-established members of the creative class could shuttle between New York and their country homes in Bucks County with ease, especially after the advent of the automobile. Art galleries sprung up in the New Hope countryside while Broadway musicals were previewed at the **Bucks County Playhouse** (a former gristmill and an active theater to this day). New Hope's artistic bent spread a bit deeper into Bucks County, which became home for celebrity personalities like Dorothy Parker and George S. Kaufman. New Hope continued to thrive as a progressive vacation town. It was among the first American getaway spots friendly to gay tourism. The town now attracts a diverse collection of visitors, from white-collar Philadelphia professionals to the teenage counterculture. Lodging options are mostly high end bed & breakfasts (more than a dozen scattered throughout town), including cozy **Lexington House** and the lavish **Inn at Bowman's Hill.** A wide variety of shops, restaurants, museums, bed & breakfasts, and nightclubs fill out Main Street. Families take themed train rides on the **New Hope & Ivyland Railroad.** Motorcyclists convene for Sunday brunch at the riverfront restaurants, and art enthusiasts peruse the galleries. A short walk across the river in New Jersey is **Lambertville,** a similarly trendy art town known for its plethora of antiques shops and Victorian architecture. Weekends around here get exceptionally crowded.

There is a lot to do in New Hope. Set aside some time to browse the unique crafts stores and stop for lunch or dinner. Homemade ice cream at

Gerenser's and fresh baked brioche at C'est La Vie bakery are inexpensive delicacies. Sit-down dining options include a litany of fancier venues like **Marsha Brown**—an excellent steakhouse occupying a converted Methodist church—and excellent New American cuisine at **Tastebuds.** Nightspots range from classic music clubs and local institutions like **John and Peter's** to recent arrivals like the **Sandbar.** A short distance off Main Street is **George Nakashima Woodworkers,** an active gallery displaying furniture designed by the late woodworker and his daughter Mira. It is open to the public on Saturday afternoons. On the historical front, **Parry Mansion** integrates four different periods' worth of furnishings into a single house tour. The Parry family helped develop the New Hope mill economy in the late 18th century when the town was known as Coryell's Ferry. In fact, it was Benjamin Parry's mill—built in 1790 to replace a structure that had been destroyed by fire 30 years earlier—that inspired the town's current name (Parry's mill being the "new hope" for the town). The Parry mill is now the Bucks County Playhouse.

Lock 12 of the Delaware Canal alongside River Road in Lumberville

Musical boulder field at Ringing Rocks Park

You'll want to stop and explore New Hope, but expect to pay for the privilege; nobody parks for free in New Hope. Every conceivable space has been painted and metered by the disarmingly attentive township bureaucrats. The only exceptions are for those staying at area bed & breakfasts, many of which allow free parking for guests. And sometimes the town covers up its meters during the holidays to encourage visitors to patronize the shopping district.

River Road winds its way out of New Hope and confronts the US 202 intersection that offers toll bridge access across the Delaware and a means to Doylestown, the Bucks County seat, located 10 miles west of the river. Continue north on PA 32; the route soon runs through **Lumberville,** an eponymous old lumber town that is as calm and reserved as New Hope is sprightly. There are two bed & breakfasts clustered around a couple stores, including the nicely renovated **Black Bass Hotel,** which reopened in June

2009. A small shoulder allows drivers to pull off and see Lock 12 of the Delaware Canal and catch a view of the New Jersey riverbanks. Soon after Lumberville comes **Point Pleasant,** inner-tube-rental capital of Pennsylvania. Point Pleasant is home base for Bucks County River Country, which shuttles tube renters upriver in school buses so they can float down the Delaware at a leisurely pace. The town's other major presence is F.P. Kolbe, a large home and garden store. Tohickon Creek, a tributary of the Delaware, flows through Point Pleasant. A couple times a year a whitewater release from Tohickon's northern end at Lake Nockamixon transforms the creek into a Class IV rapid. Scenic views of the creek can be found nearby at **Ralph Stover State Park.**

The road switches places with the towpath around **Erwinna** and moves closer to the riverbanks. A short side road leads to the hilltop Sand Castle Winery (built to resemble an actual sand castle), where the views extend for miles. River Road bends past the Golden Pheasant Inn and then EverMay on the Delaware, a once-operational bed & breakfast that one hopes might be someday restored and reopened. A bit farther down is **Tinicum Park,** which is a must-visit on Saturday afternoons (May to October) when regulation polo matches are played on the park's main field, easily accessible from River Road. It's as much fun for the polo as it is for the entertaining play-by-play announcer and the people-watching. Five dollars per car grants you entrance to the park, making Tinicum polo a bargain. Still, elements of hierarchy remain: a contingent of regulars pay an annual fee to attend matches under white tents along the far sideline.

Erwinna is a gateway to the northernmost reaches of Bucks County, where the region becomes more wholly rural. Pass through **Upper Black Eddy,** home to the excellent **Bridgeton on the Delaware** bed & breakfast and Riverview Antiques, an uncommonly interesting antiques shop with a variety of ceramics and glassware. Milford, on the New Jersey side, along with nearby Frenchtown, have more amenities than Upper Black Eddy, and both are a fine jumping-off point for exploring the New Jersey side of the Delaware. Just past the bridge connecting Upper Black Eddy to Milford is a small blue sign pointing drivers to **Ringing Rocks Park.** This side trip (roughly 2 miles off PA 32 if you follow Bridgeton Hill Road) feeds into a short trail leading to a large field of boulders. Should you happen to have a hammer or similarly weighted instrument in the car, hit a boulder with it and create a surprisingly melodic, high-pitched ringing sound (not all the rocks "ring," so you may need to try a few). It's a puzzling phenomenon.

Return to River Road and continue to through to **Kintnersville,** an early German village heavily populated with Shawnee Indians prior to white settlement. River Road feeds into PA 611 here. A worthwhile stop at Gristies Bucks County Antiques is found roadside, housed in a converted mill. The route bends through a generously plotted residential neighborhood and a rare stoplight where you'll find the Ferndale Inn, one of the better restaurants in upper Bucks. The similarly rustic town of **Revere** follows Kintnersville on PA 611 south. Swing through Revere and make a fast right turn onto Durham Road (PA 412) past Friends Pizza and Ice Cream, which happens to be a fine stop for a soft-serve cone. A short distance later, make the left onto PA 563 at the oWowCow Creamery (ice cream is big in upper Bucks) and follow this road to **Nockamixon State Park,** where the drive concludes. Pass the boat access points and make the left into the park at the main entrance by the stone park office.

You can easily spend the whole day at Nockamixon, particularly if you

Boat rentals at Lake Nockamixon

bring a rod and reel. Warm-water bass fishing is just one of several activities that attract visitors to the lush, expansive park and its 1,450-acre lake. Canoe and kayak rentals are a fun and inexpensive way to tour Lake Nockamixon, which is wrapped on all sides by parkland and inhabited by walleye, carp, and other species in addition to the bass. A swimming pool, located near the boat concession, is a good place to set up if you wish to spend the day. Picnic tables and grills are available, and the site offers easy access to the park's hiking and bike trails, which mostly cling to the lakeshore.

IN THE AREA

Accommodations

The entire Delaware River trip can be done in a single shot, though it may feel rushed. For a more relaxed visit, turn the trip into an overnight or weekend getaway. Bed & breakfasts line River Road and cluster around New Hope. Several chain hotels can also be found in Quakertown, near Nockamixon State Park.

Black Bass Hotel, 3774 River Road, Lumberville. Call 215-297-9260. Nicely renovated and auspiciously located on a serene piece of waterfront real estate. Web site: www.blackbasshotel.com.

Bridgeton on the Delaware, 1525 River Road, Upper Black Eddy. Call 610-982-5856. A beautifully appointed riverside bed & breakfast steps from the Upper Black Eddy–Milford Bridge. Some rooms overlook the Delaware, and hot breakfast can be taken on the terrace. Web site: www.bridgetonhouse.com.

Inn at Bowman's Hill, 518 Lurgan Road, New Hope. Call 215-862-8090. Luxurious New Hope accommodations featuring Egyptian cotton towels and a heated in-ground swimming pool with ample space for sunbathing. Web site: www.theinnatbowmanshill.com.

Lexington House, 6171 Upper York Road, New Hope. Call 215-794-0811. Fresh flowers accentuate the rooms and sundry plant life cover the grounds at this well-tended fieldstone inn. The Lexington is slightly removed from the bustling riverfront New Hope nightlife, allowing for privacy and quiet. Web site: www.lexingtonhouse.com.

Attractions and Recreation

Bowman's Hill Wildflower Preserve, 1635 River Road, New Hope. Call 215-862-2924. Web site: www.bhwp.org.

Bucks County Playhouse, 70 S. Main Street, New Hope. Call 215-862-2046. Web site: www.buckscountyplayhouse.com.

Bucks County River Country, 2 Walters Lane, Point Pleasant. Call 215-297-5000. Summer season is June–Aug.; call for nonsummer-season hours. Web site: www.canoeonline.com.

Delaware Canal State Park, 11 Lodi Hill Road, Upper Black Eddy. Call 610-982-5560. Web site: www.dcnr.state.pa.us/stateparks/parks/delaware canal.aspx.

George Nakashima Woodworkers, 1847 Aquetong Road, New Hope. Call 215-862-2272. Web site: www.nakashimawoodworker.com.

New Hope & Ivyland Railroad, 32 W. Bridge Street, New Hope. Call 215-862-2332. Open year-round; call ahead for trip schedules. Web site: www.newhoperailroad.com.

Nockamixon State Park, 1542 Mountain View Drive, Quakertown. Call 215-529-7300. Web site: www.dcnr.state.pa.us/stateparks/parks /nockamixon.aspx.

Parry Mansion, 45 S. Main Street, New Hope. Call 215-862-9432. Open weekends, May–Oct. Web site: www.newhopehs.org.

Pennsbury Manor, 400 Pennsbury Memorial Road, Morrisville. Call 215-946-0400. Open Tues.–Sun., year-round. Web site: www.pennsbury manor.org.

Ralph Stover State Park, Pipersville. Call 610-982-5560. Web site: www.dcnr.state.pa.us/stateparks/parks/ralphstover/ralphstover.aspx.

Ringing Rocks Park, Ringing Rocks Road, Upper Black Eddy. Call 215-757-0571.

Tinicum Park Polo Club, Tinicum Park: 972 River Road, Erwinna. Call 908-996-3321. Matches every Sat. afternoon (weather permitting), May–Oct. Web site: www.tinicumpolo.org.

Washington Crossing Historic Park, 1112 River Road, Washington Crossing. Call 215-493-4076. Visitors center open Tues.–Sun., year-round. Web site: www.ushistory.org/washingtoncrossing.

Dining and Nightlife

John and Peter's, 96 S. Main Street, New Hope. Call 215-862-5981. A storied New Hope music venue; still a fun component to a night out in New Hope. Web site: www.johnandpeters.com.

Marsha Brown, 15 S. New Hope Street, New Hope. Call 215-862-7044. A posh New Orleans–style steakhouse and gourmet dining room housed in a converted Methodist church. Can be pricey, but terrific food. Open for lunch, dinner, and Sun. brunch. Web site: www.marshabrownrestaurant .com.

Sandbar, 90 S. Main Street, New Hope. Call 215-862-3030. A little on the chicer side of New Hope's varied bar and restaurant offerings. Look for good happy hour specials. Web site: www.sandbarnewhope.com.

Tastebuds, 49 W. Ferry Street, New Hope. Call 215-862-9722. Contemporary meets rustic at this stylishly furnished 1840 building. The creative New American menu is in line with the decor. Tastebuds is also a rare New Hope BYOB. Open for dinner. Web site: www.tastebuds-newhope .com.

Yardley Inn, 82 E. Afton Avenue, Yardley. Call 215-493-3800. A very friendly atmosphere and an impressively creative New American menu. Open for lunch, dinner, and Sun. brunch. Web site: www.yardleyinn.com.

Other Contacts

Bucks County Conference and Visitors Bureau, 3207 Street Road, Bensalem. Call 215-639-0300. Web site: www.visitbuckscounty.com.

A winter view of Jim Thorpe

CHAPTER

2

A Taste of the Poconos

Estimated length: 90 miles
Estimated time: 1–2 days

Getting there: Start in Hawley, head east on US 6 briefly, and pick up PA 507 south, hugging Lake Wallenpaupack. Switch to PA 191 south in the village of Newfoundland, and take this down to Stroudsburg. From Stroudsburg, continue on PA 191 south over McMichaels Creek, and then turn left on PA 611 south. Follow 611 for 2 miles into Delaware Water Gap. After touring the Gap, turn back around, and take PA 611 north to PA 191 north. Then switch to the business route of PA 209 south and follow 209 as it hooks west into Jim Thorpe.

Highlights: This sweeping journey around the Pocono Mountains offers a glimpse into Pennsylvania's ever-changing tourist economy and the natural scenery of the northeast, hitting major Pocono attractions like Lake Wallenpaupack and popular weekend getaway towns like Stroudsburg, Delaware Water Gap, and Jim Thorpe.

As long as there have been cities, there have been country escapes. Well before the Industrial Revolution shrouded manufacturing cities like New York and Philadelphia in soot, those who could afford it looked for clean air and open spaces in the not-too-distant countryside. New Yorkers headed to the Catskill Mountains and Bostonians to shore resorts like Cape Cod or Newport. Philadelphians had the Poconos.

The Pocono region is a 2,400-square-mile area spread across several northeastern Pennsylvania counties. Its name is derived from the Lenape phrase "stream between two mountains," which refers to the local segment of the Delaware River. The river up here bears little resemblance to the Delaware that feeds Philadelphia's port a hundred miles south. This is a clean, placid waterway that supports smallmouth bass, shad, and catfish.

In his excellent book *Better in the Poconos,* historian Lawrence Squeri observes that the social character of Philadelphia extends neatly into its country getaway. The early, privatist instincts of Philadelphia's upper class kept the Poconos well insulated from all but a moneyed elite. While the Catskill resorts were similarly exclusive in their infancy, the region evolved into a much larger, more diverse, and more egalitarian vacation destination. Nothing like the Borscht Belt ever existed in the Poconos, even as it slowly grew out of its early iteration as an exclusive Protestant retreat.

The original Pocono lodges sprouted up during the first half of the 19th century in Monroe and Pike counties—towns like Delaware Water Gap, Stroudsburg, and Milford absorbed some tourist business to complement the fishing, farming, and tanning economy that predominated. Stagecoaches brought Philadelphians to the Poconos as a way to escape the swampy realities of summer in the city. Hiking, fishing, hunting, and swimming were common recreational pastimes, though many visitors were content to rest and enjoy the solitude. Quaker ethos favored propriety and quiet spiritual renewal. And while not all early visitors were Quaker, the other well-represented sects (Methodist and Presbyterian) were hardly bohemian.

As with so much of Pennsylvania, the railroads brought considerable changes. The opening of completed passenger lines in the mid-1850s meant greater accessibility—not only for Philadelphians, but also vacationers from New York and budding industrial cities like Allentown in the Lehigh Valley. Resorts grew larger and more lavish. Gourmet menus appeared in the dining rooms. During the region's gravy days in the early 20th century, Monroe and Pike counties offered dozens of resorts that catered to an increasingly diverse clientele. Meanwhile, the tourist business expanded north into lower Wayne County and west into Carbon County.

After this large, early-20th-century boom in tourist traffic, the Poconos settled down. The Depression naturally weakened the market for luxury vacations. The interstate highway system injected some new activity in the post–World War II era, but these gains were offset by the increasing affordability of air travel and the requisite accessibility of the Sunbelt, Europe, and the Caribbean islands. But the Poconos soldiered on, recasting itself as a honeymooners' paradise (the heart-shaped Jacuzzi retains a close identification with the region) and later as a premier skiing destination. Outlet shopping in Tannersville, family fun at the **Skytop Lodge,** and a Las Vegas–style casino resort complete the fuzzy picture of what a "Poconos getaway" is today. In truth, it can be many things, from a weekend of spa treatments to a harrowing journey down the slopes. The natural beauty is still there, and summer in the Poconos offers many of the same opportunities that first attracted Philadelphia gentlemen in the 1800s—hills blanketed in mountain laurel, densely wooded spruce forests for hiking, quiet streams for fishing, and thousands of acres of game lands. All within a two-hour drive of Philadelphia, northern New Jersey, or New York City.

The region's proximity to Manhattan has had another effect. Rising land prices and sprawl throughout the New York metropolitan area convinced a number of former city dwellers and suburbanites to move their primary residences to northeastern Pennsylvania during the late 1990s and early 2000s. There is much to be said for the tranquility, despite the commute. A 2007 article in *The New Yorker* magazine profiled a legal secretary who travels three hours and fifteen minutes each way from a ranch-style house in Pike County to Manhattan. Her meticulously documented trip (a half-hour car ride, plus two commuter trains and a subway) betrays a dash of eccentricity but also the desirability of living in the Poconos.

Things have cooled off a bit since the housing bubble popped in 2008, but locals remain keenly attuned to the real estate market. A delicate balance endures between new residents, old residents, commuters, and vacationers. Monroe County is by and large at peace with the tourist economy; friendly small towns like Stroudsburg and Delaware Water Gap support sizable year-round communities and welcome visitors with open arms. Sentiments elsewhere can be different.

There are many ways to drive around the Poconos. The region is webbed by scenic state roads and interstate highways. This drive is intended as a Poconos primer, open to deviation and adjustment. Ski enthusiasts, gamblers, and outlet shoppers may have their own ideas. For those who like to make it up as they go along, the Pocono Mountains Visitors Bureau does a great job papering the hot spots with maps and visitor information. There is also a state-of-the-art visitors center just outside Delaware Water Gap, opened in 2006.

Begin in **Hawley,** the drive's northernmost point, and the gateway to **Lake Wallenpaupack** on the border between Pike and Wayne counties. The lake is a renowned recreational destination, built in the mid-1920s to provide hydroelectric power, just as it does today in a more limited capacity. For a time it was the largest man-made lake in the state. It has always been popular for sailing and fishing—Wallenpaupack and her creeks support bass, trout, and pickerel. Hawley, a modestly sized old lumber and mill town just 3 miles north of the lake, now serves the tourist trade with lodging and restaurants. Remnants of its industrial character remain—one of Hawley's former mills (a magnificent bluestone castle that spun silk and textiles until its 1986 shutdown) is in the final stages of a conversion from industrial facility into the anchor space for a local branch of Lackawanna College.

Hawley's compact downtown is separated somewhat from US 6. Stop in at the Lunchbox Café or Hawley Diner on Main Avenue before a morning on the lake and have them pack wraps and sandwiches to go. For a fine sit-down meal, head to the bank building that accommodates the town's premier gourmet restaurant, **Torte Knox.** There are also a few interesting stores, like Jukebox Classics and Vintage Slot Machines, Inc., which is fun to browse if you're into old neon signs and the like.

The short drive from Hawley to the lake is punctuated by the Lake Wallenpaupack Visitors Center, which is situated just north of the US 6/PA 507 intersection. There is a small parking lot here, which feeds into an entry point for the 1.5-mile nature trail that wraps around the lake's northern end. Alternating between wood chip surfacing and gravel, the trail is a perfect way to explore the lake banks and the public beach area (swimming is $3 for adults, $1 for children). The route ends at the actual dam, tightly guarded by the Pennsylvania Power & Light Corporation.

You could easily spend a week or more at Lake Wallenpaupack, camping, fishing, sailing, and exploring. The drive down PA 507, which follows the eastern shore, is filled with people who do just that; private houses, time-shares, cottages, and retreats fill out much of the lakefront real estate. Wallenpaupack's south end is notable for its public access and campsites.

Pass under I-84 and through **Newfoundland,** a quiet little town with a couple restaurants. PA 507 merges with PA 191 south here, so make the switch. This segment of the drive is a window into the Poconos' artisan tra-

All quiet at Lake Wallenpaupack

ditions—there's Wildlife Arts, a workshop and gallery in **South Sterling** that features attractive animal carvings made from unusual woods, and then **La Anna**'s famous Holley Ross Pottery. In addition to the 22-karat gold-plated pottery made on-site, Holley Ross sells hard to find imported pieces and novelties, including an eye-catching selection of Polish pottery. Behind the factory (where you might catch a morning pottery demonstration) is a compact park area known as the Swinging Bridge Lake & Forest, which is great for picnicking so long as the gnats stay away. A short nature trail and lake round out the Holley Ross experience.

Portions of 191 are delightfully secluded, offering a peek into what the Pocono Mountains looked like before the tourism boom. Occasional restaurants and country shops add to the scenery. The town of **Mountain-**

Car show in downtown Stroudsburg

home has a great soft-pretzel purveyor in Callie's Pretzel Factory. And life imitates art at the Left Handed Souvenir store (recall Ned Flanders's *Simpsons* conceit), which is part of Callie's and sells mugs, pens, and other novelties made for southpaws. The next village over is **Cresco,** an early-20th-century hunting and fishing hot spot. The local township restored Cresco's old hunter green Delaware Lackawanna & Western Railroad train station (a key artery through which the area's tourist traffic once flowed), stocking it with local treasures and converting it into the **Cresco Station Museum.** The museum and Homestead Inn restaurant are located just beyond Cresco's main drag, where you'll find shops like A Trunk in the Attic (a small indoor flea market).

The ups and downs grow steeper as PA 191 meets PA 940 at the Crescent Lodge and Country Inn. Make the left to stay on 191 and continue through to Skywood Park, which offers a creative fitness trail and gorgeous views. You're in the vicinity of **Paradise Valley,** where the trout fishing comes in both organic and inorganic settings; organic at Paradise Creek, which parallels this section of the route, and inorganic at the Paradise Trout Hatchery. A low entrance fee gets you access to the well-stocked hatchery ponds. Of course, fishing is much easier here than in the creek, but you'll have to pay for anything you catch.

Just a couple miles down the road from the hatchery is a real blast from the past. Assuming it's still standing, pull over and take a gander at the Penn Hills Resort, a once proud Poconos getaway spot whose baby-boom-era design and decor are an oasis of anachronism amid the modern Pocono Mountains and the luxury resorts nearby. The Penn Hills finally closed in 2009 after years of neglect. At press time the property was being readied for a tax sale; its future uncertain, the Penn Hills nurses a cool ghost town vibe. You can almost see Mike and Carol Brady volleying on the overgrown tennis courts.

A return to 21st-century civilization comes in the form of **Stroudsburg.** A fun little Poconos village that evolved from mill town into tourist hot spot during the region's heyday, Stroudsburg maintains much of the buoyancy that has attracted summer guests and weekenders for more than a century. Stroudsburg's unusually wide Main Street sports a fair share of pubs, restaurants (give **Siamsa** a try), and sporting goods stores, as well as a robust schedule of public events on weekends. Just down the street is Dunkelberger's, a clothing and outdoorsman's spot that's like a great army-navy surplus store. It's also a perfect place to pick up gear for fishing in the streams that partially enclose the central business district. And if it seems mysterious to smell tobacco wafting out of the J.J. Newberry's five and dime department store, that's because the flagship property of the now-defunct chain has been converted into an Atlantic Cigar shop.

Just 2 miles east is **Delaware Water Gap**. This small riverside town lies on the Pennsylvania side of the Delaware River between Mount Minsi and New Jersey's Mount Tammany. The formation is an overwhelming, beautiful piece of geography, and it's easy to see why elite Philadelphians began flocking here in the mid-19th century. This is pretty much where the Poconos got their start—where ambitious French speculator Antoine

Dutot began erecting the region's first hotel in 1829. He ran out of money before the building was completed and his self-referential name for the town ("Dutotsburg") didn't stick, but the place came to life years after his death. The lodge he'd begun building became the mammoth Kittatinny Hotel, the first major Poconos resort. At its Roaring Twenties peak, the town supported 50 such hotels and catered to a wide array of visitors. All but one of the old resorts (the venerable **Deer Head Inn**) has been lost, many to insurance fires (the Depression-era bust predated the advent of bankruptcy laws). But the Gap's founder remains a presence at the **Antoine Dutot Museum and Gallery**—a converted schoolhouse and an enlightening peek into Poconos history. The permanent collection on the second floor includes old postcards, resort advertisements, Indian arrowheads, and other Americana like an outmoded coffee grinder and crank telephone. The first floor features work by local artists.

Another way to experience this history is to take a **Delaware Water Gap Trolley Tour** ($10 for adults) in a replica vehicle modeled after the trolleys that once escorted schoolchildren and tourists up and down the village's steep mountain curves. Drivers are local guides, well versed in the Gap's folklore, and pop off stories about the iconoclasts and celebrities who used to hang around during the vacation season. There's also the more alarming recent history—three massive, punishing floods have assaulted the Gap over the last decade.

The trolley tour also makes a stop at PA 611 near the site of the old Kittatinny Hotel. This is the narrowest and therefore windiest point in the Gap. The scenery is great here: the New Jersey side has a popular sand beach along the Delaware in the shadows of 1,500-foot-high Mount Tammany. Look for hikers attempting to scale the whole thing. PA 611 is also where you'll find roadside "Cold Air Cave," where 38-degree air flows from an opening in Mount Minsi.

Once you're done exploring Delaware Water Gap, proceed to the PA 209 business route south. The towns of **Snydersville** and **Sciota** will appear after the PA 33 intersection. You may wish to make a roadside stop at Brinker's Mill (labeled THE OLD MILL) in Sciota, a small, 250-year-old fieldstone gristmill that helped store supplies for the Continental Army in 1779 during Gen. John Sullivan's 1779 march across the northern Pennsylvania tier into western New York. The march occurred at a critical moment in the American Revolution, when Iroquois tribes allied with the British and loyalist colonists were proving themselves an increasingly effective opponent of the Continental Army. Sullivan and his men were charged with laying waste to the region's Iroquois villages, killing as many Iroquois as possible and demoralizing the people. You'll see many historical markers noting Sullivan's March along the next two drives, both of which cover Iroquois territory Sullivan destroyed on his way to western New York. But this simple little mill suggests none of that mayhem. It's a rather quiet, countrified place to fish or catch a creek view off the restored bridge.

The business route rejoins US 209 just outside Sciota. This portion of 209 is dotted with ice cream shops and nurseries. It weaves past towns like **Broadheadsville**—communities organized around large land plots and intermittent development that fashions a quasi-rural, quasi-suburban

Sandy beach at Beltzville State Park

character. A steep downgrade from these towns approaches the I-476 crossover. Take a short side trip (3 miles) off 209 at the crossover to **Beltzville State Park.** This is a particularly good idea in the summer; the park sports an unusually large sand beach that abuts 949-acre Beltzville Lake. Boat rentals, fishing, and hiking are other possibilities.

US 209 around the I-476 crossover is a heavily commercialized area due to the presence of the interstate exit (a gateway into the Poconos for many visitors). Pass the chain restaurants and hotels and take the route deeper into Carbon County. An optional turnoff to the **Lehighton** business district reveals a sturdy blue collar town, its core streets lined by hardware stores and frame houses. One terrific stop is the Lehighton Bakery and its renowned Pershing doughnut—a sweet treat topped with thick, buttery frosting and raspberry jelly. After Lehighton, return to 209 and follow it the rest of the way up the mountainside. A couple miles later you'll coast down into **Jim Thorpe.** This beautiful little village (dubbed the Switzerland of America during its industrial-era heyday) is blessed with an idyllic location amid rolling mountains on the banks of the Lehigh River. The natural scenery is enhanced by neat rows of colorfully accented Victorian homes and hillside mansions. At its peak, during the coal and railroad boom of the 1870s, the town became a haven for the extraordinarily affluent—a majority of American millionaires owned a mansion here. Recent decades have brought substantial wealth into Jim Thorpe once again, allowing for impressive restoration efforts.

Like many other villages around the region, Jim Thorpe runs on tourism. But its history follows a very different path than that of Strouds-burg and Delaware Water Gap. Unlike these early tourist hot spots, Jim Thorpe's initial development was fueled by coal. The seat of Carbon County, it boomed during the early 19th century as East Coast metropolises required an increasingly large amount of Pennsylvania anthracite to power its factories and homes. Its evolution into a thriving tourist spot occurred only a couple decades ago, and its roots have much more in common with the coal towns profiled in the next chapter than with the rest of the Poconos' vacation towns. A 15,000-pound hunk of anthracite in the town square pays tribute to this history. Of course, Lenape settlements predated the coal boom. The town was known as Mauch Chunk (pronounced "Mock Chunk")—a Lenape term meaning "mountain of sleeping bear"—until 1954, when it was controversially changed to Jim Thorpe, after the great Native American athlete.

It's not as though Mauch Chunk wanted for historical interest and import prior to its incarnation as Jim Thorpe. The town was thoroughly involved with the development of coal transport technology—in 1827 it became one end of the Switchback gravity railroad, which brought anthracite from the mountains into Mauch Chunk at speeds approaching 50 miles per hour (tourists were invited to ride the Switchback when it wasn't hauling coal). Two years later the Lehigh Canal completed the chain, connecting Mauch Chunk with Easton and the lucrative markets accessible via the Delaware River and its canal (see chapter 1). Canals later gave way to railroads, and Mauch Chunk became a stop on the Lehigh Valley railroad as well as home to its founder, Asa Packer.

Packer's fortune bought him an exceptional house. You'll want to visit the **Asa Packer Mansion** and experience all that a Gilded Age mansion can be, from the crystal and blue glass chandeliers to the rosettes hand-carved into the main hallway trim (no two alike) to the curios Asa's daughter Mary brought back to Mauch Chunk from her 17 (yes, 17) trips around the world. Guided tours take approximately one hour, though there's so much to see you feel like you've barely gotten a taste. Next door is the **Harry Packer Mansion,** an equally ornate redbrick house built by Asa for his youngest son. The Harry Packer house is now a popular bed & breakfast, and the ground floor is open for self guided tours—note the three stained-glass windows in the dining room, each designed to represent a meal of the day. The veranda overlooks Jim Thorpe and is open to the public as a lounge. It's a nice spot to enjoy a glass of wine.

The Packer mansions are located just up the hill from the base of the town near the old Mauch Chunk railroad station. The station doubles as a visitors center for Jim Thorpe and is stocked with tourism information and a brief overview of the local history. You may wish to take a train trip along the Lehigh River on the **Lehigh Gorge Scenic Railway**—trains leave from

WHAT'S IN A NAME?

Mauch Chunk's name change to Jim Thorpe was the result of a bizarre transaction between town elders and Patricia Thorpe—widow of Jim Thorpe—who agreed to have Thorpe's remains exhumed and transferred from Oklahoma to Carbon County. Residents built a new resting place for the trailblazing football player and Olympic athlete, looking to draw attention to what had become a postindustrial town in decline. Discord surrounded the name change at the time, and it persists to this day.

the Mauch Chunk Station, once part of the Jersey Central (a competitor of Packer's Lehigh Valley Railroad). A good way to explore the town on foot is to begin here and work your way up Broadway, past the **Inn at Jim Thorpe,** where many shops, restaurants, entertainment venues, museums, and galleries are located. History buffs will want to check out the **Mauch Chunk Museum & Cultural Center,** which features a large model of the Switchback gravity railroad and a thorough presentation on Jim Thorpe's evolution from coal town to vacation hot spot. A fair distance up the hill is the **Old Jail Museum,** a true must-see. This eerie stone structure, replete with dungeon cells in the basement, was a functioning jail as recently as 1995. More than a hundred years prior, seven of the Molly Maguires—the famous Irish coal miners who resisted the exploitation of their labors by purportedly violent means—were hanged at the jail's gallows. (For more on the Molly Maguires, consult chapter 3.)

Jim Thorpe's resurgence as a tourist destination is grounded in a genuinely diverse appeal. Restaurants on and around Broadway, like the **Albright Mansion,** cater mostly to professional couples who come here to relax, peruse the shops, and possibly investigate the local history. There is also an artistic bent to the town. Local musicians can be found all around Jim Thorpe, sometimes in public spaces, other times at small private venues and coffeehouses. The historic **Mauch Chunk Opera House** is one of several popular places to see live music in Jim Thorpe. Built in 1881, the 390-seat facility made its name hosting vaudeville stage shows and now presents a diverse lineup of rock, blues, jazz, and country bands, as well as occasional tribute performances. Look for big name acts appearing at **Penn's Peak** (four times the opera house's size), which is located a few miles northeast of downtown. The art scene is alive as well, and local artists have several galleries' worth of space to show their work.

Recreational enthusiasts of all skill levels are also drawn to Jim Thorpe. The raft-, kayak-, and bike-rental concessions clustered around the outdoorsman shops at the base of the town near the railroad station and plaza serve the multitudes who use Jim Thorpe as a jumping-off point to float down the Lehigh River or bike down the Lehigh Gorge Rail Trail through **Lehigh Gorge State Park**—a mostly flat ride incorporating the valley's lush scenery and what's left of the coal-era infrastructure. Up the mountainside in the opposite direction is man-made Mauch Chunk Lake, a favorite campsite and swimming attraction.

IN THE AREA

Accommodations

There's no shortage of lodging options in the Poconos, from luxury resorts and time-shares to campgrounds and cabin rentals around Lake Wallenpaupack.

Deer Head Inn, 5 Main Street, Delaware Water Gap. Call 570-424-2000. This Victorian-style throwback (formerly the Central House) is the last remaining of the original Delaware Water Gap resorts that filled out the town during the Poconos' glory days. The Deer Head is best known for its jazz club, which heats up Thurs.–Sun. Web site: www.deerheadinn.com.

Harry Packer Mansion, 1 Packer Hill Road, Jim Thorpe. Call 570-325-8566. If the place looks familiar, it's because this ornate Gilded Age palace was the inspiration for Disney World's Haunted Mansion ride. All-inclusive murder-mystery weekends run $500–600 per couple and incorporate an interactive whodunit into your stay. Web site: www.murdermansion.com.

The Inn at Jim Thorpe, 24 Broadway, Jim Thorpe. Call 570-325-2599. Affordable accommodations centrally located in downtown Jim Thorpe. Forty-five rooms make up this elegantly decorated, 160-year-old Victorian-style hotel marked by a cast-iron balcony that evokes the French Quarter. Web site: www.innjt.com.

Skytop Lodge, 1 Skytop Lodge, Skytop. Call 570-595-7401. A popular family resort located a few miles north of Mountainhome, Skytop is big on wintertime sports, with skiing, ice skating, and even dogsledding all available on-site. Golf and hiking are warmer-weather attractions. Room rates include three meals daily per guest. Web site: www.skytop.com.

Attractions and Recreation

Antoine Dutot Museum and Gallery, Main Street, Delaware Water Gap. Call 570-476-4240. Open weekends, May–Oct. Web site: www.dutot museum.com.

Asa Packer Mansion Museum, Packer Road, Jim Thorpe. Call 570-325-8566. Open weekends in Apr., May, Nov., and early Dec.; open daily June–Oct. Web site: www.asapackermansion.com.

Beltzville State Park, 2950 Pohopoco Drive, Leighton. Call 610-377-0045. Web site: www.dcnr.state.pa.us/stateparks/parks/beltzville.aspx.

Cresco Station Museum, Route 390 and Sand Spring Road, Cresco. Call 570-595-2279. Open Wed. and Sat. afternoons in July and Aug.; Sun. only in June, Sept., and Oct.

Delaware Water Gap Trolley Tour, Main Street, Delaware Water Gap. Call 570-476-9766. Web site: www.watergaptrolley.com.

Lehigh Gorge Scenic Railway, Mauch Chunk train station, downtown Jim Thorpe. Call 570-325-8485. Open May–Dec.; call ahead for trip schedules. Web site: www.lgsry.com.

Lehigh Gorge State Park, White Haven. Call 570-443-0400. Web site: www.dcnr.state.pa.us/stateparks/parks/lehighgorge.aspx.

Mauch Chunk Museum & Cultural Center, 41 W. Broadway, Jim Thorpe. Call 570-325-9190. Open Tues.–Sun., year-round. Web site: www.mauchchunkmuseum.com.

Mauch Chunk Opera House, 14 W. Broadway, Jim Thorpe. Call 570-325-0249. Web site: www.mauchchunkoperahouse.com.

Old Jail Museum, 128 W. Broadway, Jim Thorpe. Call 570-325-5259. Open Thurs.–Tues., May–Sept.; weekends only in Sept. and Oct. Web site: www.theoldjailmuseum.com.

Penn's Peak, 325 Maury Road, Jim Thorpe. Call 610-826-9000. Web site: www.pennspeak.com.

Dining and Nightlife

Albright Mansion, 66 Broadway, Jim Thorpe. Call 570-325-4400. This English-themed restaurant serves three meals a day and high tea complete with clotted cream imported from Devon. Web site: www.albrightmansion.org.

Siamsa, 636 Main Street, Stroudsburg. Call 570-421-8434. A terrific Irish pub, built in Ireland, then imported and assembled on-site. Shepherd's pie is a highlight, as is the onion soup. Open for lunch, dinner, and Sun. brunch. Web site: www.siamsairishpub.com.

Torte Knox, 301 Main Avenue, Hawley. Call 570-226-8200. The quality of the cuisine has made a name for Torte Knox throughout the Poconos as well as among urban foodies in Manhattan and Philadelphia. Consider registering for a popular evening cooking class. Also an excellent choice for a gourmet brunch before a day at the lake. Open for lunch, dinner, and Sun. brunch. Web site: www.torteknox.com.

Other Contacts

Pocono Mountains Visitors Bureau, 1004 Main Street, Stroudsburg. Call 800-762-6667. Web site: www.800poconos.com.

Turntable at Steamtown National Historic Site

CHAPTER

3

Anthracite Country

Estimated length: 105 miles
Estimated time: 1–2 days

Getting there: From Honesdale, follow US 6 west. Switch to US 6 Business Route west just outside of Carbondale and follow through the city center toward Scranton. Switch to US 11 south near Scranton. Follow US 11 south through Pittston, along the Susquehanna River, all the way to Bloomsburg. Past the Bloomsburg business district, switch to PA 42 south to Centralia.

Highlights: A drive through northeast Pennsylvania's coal country decades after the industry's peak, this tour delves into anthracite's history and the varied ways in which this beautiful corner of the state has adjusted to economic circumstance. The trip incorporates old coal towns like Scranton and Pittston, charming Bloomsburg, and finishes up in the mostly abandoned (and still smoldering) town of Centralia. Short recreational side trips include Lackawanna State Forest and Knoebels Amusement Park.

Consider the War of 1812—largely forgotten by all except military buffs and American eighth-graders the night before a history midterm. Lacking moral clarity, the conflict served mostly to revisit animosities between Great Britain and the United States still lingering from the American Revolution. But for eastern Pennsylvania, the war shaped the future more than any event since the Carboniferous Period, 300 million years prior.

The war stalled trade with England, which at the time was a major coal exporter to the young republic. This forced Americans to look locally for new energy sources and turned excavators on to the vast reserves of anthracite coal hidden beneath the Wyoming Valley soil in northeast Pennsylvania. Once the coal was discovered, financiers and engineers pieced together a canal and railroad system over subsequent decades that cast the die for the entire mid-Atlantic region.

Anthracite is hard coal—a higher-energy, cleaner burning product than the softer bituminous variety that is found in the southwest quadrant of the state and neighboring West Virginia (bituminous coal was also imported from England prior to the war). From the early 19th century onward, King Coal spawned towns up and down northeast Pennsylvania, where veins of anthracite flowed from the hills to major population centers like New York and Philadelphia.

So much of Pennsylvania's history stems from its rich and diverse portfolio of natural resources. Subsequent chapters in this book highlight the role that timber, oil, natural gas, and metals played in developing its towns and cities. But in a sense, coal made everything else possible. Not only was it discovered early on, but its presence in the Pennsylvania mountains laid the groundwork for nearly all the heavy industry that followed. Converting ore into pig iron made economic sense in Pennsylvania because the production process ran on coal; Wyoming Valley furnaces could burn around the clock on anthracite. The need to move coal across the state created a market for canals and railroads. And where better to produce those steel rails than the transportation hub of the entire region?

If coal made other industrial progress possible, it also shaped the state's social history. The first wave of English, Welsh, and Scots-Irish immigration preceded the coal boom. But these early immigrants who settled Pennsylvania's cities and farmlands were followed by a wave of Irish immigration and the blooming of anthracite country. Famine back home brought thousands of Irish coal miners to the anthracite region in the 1850s. The Irish were soon followed by Italians, Poles, Slovaks, and Hungarians, who settled dozens of coal towns around northeast Pennsylvania. Tightly knit Italian and Polish communities like Pittston and Nanticoke made anthracite country home for thousands of immigrant families. Meanwhile, as mining grew profitable, landholders and coal executives formed a white-collar professional class around the region's major population centers.

Coal mining is enormously taxing work and was even worse in the 19th century before labor laws prevented the most egregious practices. Children began working in the mines as early as eight or nine years old as "breakers" who picked at the anthracite to eliminate impurities and produce usable lumps. Mine fires, runaway coal cars, and collapsing mine shafts claimed limbs and lives. Disability benefits and survivors insurance were nonexistent. Those who worked in the coalfields for more than a few years often developed black lung. These conditions (not to mention the inconsistent hours and low pay) helped make anthracite mining ripe for labor unrest.

During the early industrial era, most Irish miners were bossed by English supervisors, and the resentments ran deep. One consequence was the formation of the Molly Maguires—a band of Irish American miners who sabotaged mine operations and murdered foremen in opposition to labor abuses and conscription into the Union army. Twenty members were hanged after an undercover operation organized by Reading Railroad president and mine owner Frank Gowen. The Molly Maguires remain controversial to this day. Some regard them as terrorists, others as heroes who were smeared for standing up to an exploitive system. Their story plays as such great narrative that it has been difficult to separate the legend from the reality. Newspapers in the 1870s erred on the side of sensationalism and many stoked an anti-immigrant bias, so conflicting accounts over the organization's actual activities and influence have muddied the historical record. Regardless, the region's labor movement was mainstreamed a decade later—the United Mine Workers of America (UMWA) formed in Ohio in 1890 and soon set up shop in anthracite country. The UMWA organized a famous coal strike in 1902, which resulted in wage increases and a nine-hour workday.

Anthracite production peaked around 1920, at which point the industry fell victim to the increasing popularity and decreasing cost of oil. The Great Depression exacerbated things considerably. During the 1930s, coal miners in the anthracite region often found only a couple days a week worth of work, which fueled both antagonism toward the industry and dissension within the union ranks. In 1935, dissident miners formed the United Anthracite Miners (UAM) of Pennsylvania to oppose what they viewed as corruption and neglect in the UMWA. Discord within the union and reduced demand for anthracite remained nagging problems for the region, though nothing was nearly as detrimental or tragic as the 1959 Knox Mine disaster near Pittston, which claimed a dozen lives.

Today's anthracite industry is barely a shadow of its former self; fewer than a thousand anthracite miners now work the northeast Pennsylvania mountains. Coal remains an important American energy source, but anthracite reserves are largely depleted, and American coal comes mostly from states like West Virginia and Wyoming. Working the mines remains a difficult way to earn a living. Sons and daughters of coal miners have large-ly moved on and moved out, accepting the industry's long, gradual decline without too much resentment. For many children of anthracite country, dif-ficult low-wage labor has given way to prosperity. Of course you can still visit the deactivated Lackawanna Coal Mine or tour Scranton's Anthracite Heritage Museum, but these attractions are intended to contextualize the history and do little to place coal in the region's present or future.

So what remains of anthracite country? Quite a lot, as a matter of fact. Put all visions of ravaged coal mountains aside—this is a scenic route, dip-ping down from the Moosic Mountains region through the Wyoming Val-ley along the North Branch of the Susquehanna River. Occasional strip malls are unavoidable along the first two thirds of the route, as this remains a populated area with suburban neighborhoods branched across the valley. The PA 42 segment has a more secluded character. There is the history too, which comes alive in the museums and monuments as well as in the pizze-rias and pubs along US 11. If your sensibilities don't require the postcard-ready towns of the Poconos, you'll feel altogether welcome in anthracite country.

This drive begins in Wayne County's **Honesdale**—a major hub of coal transport that owes its name to a New York City mayor and its early rele-vance to a Philadelphia dry goods merchant. The merchant was William Wurts, an earlier promoter of anthracite whose dogged pursuit of coal in northeast Pennsylvania set off the postwar boom. Wurts founded the Delaware and Hudson Canal Company (the "D&H") in 1825 to transport his anthracite to New York City. Thousands of mostly Irish and German immigrants spent three years digging the 108-mile canal from present-day Honesdale to port towns in upstate New York, where coal was then shipped down the Hudson River to Manhattan. Wurts also constructed a railroad connecting the anthracite-rich mountains to Honesdale: the first segment of the supply chain, and a highly speculative venture for its time. But his investments paid off. The D&H became America's first million-dollar company, and its major stockholder became its president. That man was Philip Hone, the future mayor of New York, for whom Honesdale is named.

A bucolic mountainside village, Honesdale has retained its charm even as its essentiality to the coal economy recedes into Pennsylvania's memory. Convenient to recreationalists from New York and Philadelphia, the town has benefitted from a somewhat remote location on the northeast edge of anthracite country. Honesdale remains the seat of rural Wayne County, popular with nature-seeking adventurers and adolescents who descend on the region's summer camps every June. The **Wayne County Historical Society** in central Honesdale is a good primer on the anthracite history, particularly as related to the founding and early activities of the D&H. A replicated Stourbridge Lion—the famed steam engine brought over from England to pull coal cars into Honesdale—is on display here, along with historical material on anthracite's role in growing the region and America.

Follow US 6 west out of Honesdale. It's a scenic, undulating 14-mile drive from here to hardscrabble **Carbondale,** which, as the city name suggests, was similarly central to anthracite country. Switch to the US 6 Business Route just outside Carbondale to access the 9,200-person city's downtown. You can still see the old D&H offices here (the Penn Division Headquarters), which occupied an 1832 building that has taken on new life as the Ben-Mar, among the better restaurants in Carbondale. Coal's demise is regrettably apparent in what was once a booming city engaged in all facets of the coal economy. While disinvestment and population loss has left downtown somewhat sparse, there are notable structures and indications of rebirth. One of several remarkable buildings is the Romanesque Revival–style city hall, which incorporates the police department headquarters and a transportation museum. And while downtown contains both well-maintained and poorly aged blocks, attractively landscaped residential areas fan into the city's outer ring.

Take the US 6 Business Route west out of Carbondale—this segment is also known as the Scranton-Carbondale Highway. The drive between these two coal towns hovers high over the valley. Sweeping views of the mountains and towns below are a contrast to the litany of billboards and stores that fill out the immediate landscape. Pass the diners and shopping plazas and look for **Archbald Pothole State Park,** which is located midway between the two cities on the south side of the route near a sprawling car dealership. The draw here is the 38-foot deep pothole, a natural phenomenon created by a swirling flow of water and rock that essentially drilled through the earth some ten to thirty thousand years ago. The resultant glacial pothole was found during mine excavation activities in 1884 and has been preserved. It is the centerpiece of the small park, which also offers a short hiking trail. After the pothole, proceed west, as the road continues twisting its way into higher altitudes before a descent into Scranton. If you take the route at night, you'll have the chance to visit the **Circle Drive In** movie theater—2 miles east of Scranton, the Circle shows first-run movies Friday, Saturday, and Sunday from April through September. During daylight hours on Sunday, a 50 cent admission fee gets you into a pretty good flea market.

Approaching **Scranton,** switch onto US 11 and follow the local highway into downtown. Scranton is an interesting little city and well worth a visit. With just more than 70,000 residents, its population has shrunk to half of what it was during anthracite's heyday, but a revival over the last few years has put it back on the map. There is an unpretentious intimacy to Scranton. While its manageable city center remains true to Scranton's blue-collar roots, it also shows off some jewels, like the magnificently restored neoclassical **Lackawanna Railroad Station** (now a Radisson hotel) and a stylish downtown courthouse with limestone trim. The dining scene features notables like **Carmen's Restaurant and Wine Bar** at the Radisson and comfort food from the Far East at **Thai Rak Thai.**

Should you arrive at night, it won't take long to notice the flashing bulbs atop downtown's Scranton Electric Building—one of several good-looking beaux-arts structures in the area—proclaiming Scranton's identity as THE ELECTRIC CITY. This is a well-earned boast. Scranton's streetcars ran on the first completely electrified system in America, opened in 1886 to shuttle residents between downtown and its Green Ridge neighborhood (other cities gradually integrated electric trolleys into a horse-drawn system). The streetcars are no more, having been replaced by buses and cars, but you can get a taste of the old romance at the **Electric City Trolley Museum.** Learn about the inner workings of a substation, step into a restored Scranton trolley, or admire the stained-glass windows on an elegant Philadelphia & Western Birney car. The attraction also takes you through the history of Scranton by following its transit system. As conditions improved in the coal mines and unionized workers enjoyed more generous salaries and some well-earned leisure time, the route map expanded to link suburban neighborhoods. Amusement parks and recreation areas sprouted up alongside the tracks.

The Romanesque Revival Lackawanna County Courthouse, Scranton

The trolley museum shares a parking lot with the **Steamtown National Historic Site,** on the west side of town. Steamtown is a comprehensive look at the region's railroads, complete with functioning roundhouse. A creative video presentation dramatizes the Delaware, Lackawanna & Western Railroad's importance to the valley and calls to mind the romance of passenger travel during the railroad's heyday. The economic development folks ever-consciously placed a large shopping mall right next door.

Behind the Radisson is what's left of the Scranton Iron Furnaces. This heap of heavy stone now sits peacefully by a brook but was once a small piece of a much larger Lackawanna Iron & Steel Company facility. It's a national historic park site, so you'll find panels explaining the finer points of pig iron production and the furnaces' noteworthiness. Other Scranton attractions are the aforementioned **Anthracite Heritage Museum** and the unique **Houdini Museum,** which pays tribute to history's greatest skeptic.

For better or worse, Scranton's reputation now rests partly on the shoulders of the hit NBC sitcom *The Office.* As a postindustrial city coping with 21st-century economic realities, Scranton works perfectly as a backdrop for the show's fictional Dunder Mifflin paper company. The show pokes some gentle fun at Scranton but is ultimately an enthusiastic endorsement of the city; despite their eccentricities, the company's Scranton employees possess a basic decency and warmth (notably lacking at Dunder Mifflin's corporate headquarters in Manhattan, which are rife with mismanagement and waste). Consequently, the city has embraced its identification with *The Office.* Visitors can take guided fan tours of the city that hit local hot spots like Poor Richard's Pub. And the **Mall at Steamtown** now features an entire *Office* souvenir store for those who've always wanted a Dwight Schrute bobblehead doll or "World's Best Boss" mug.

Follow US 11 south from Scranton. The 10 miles between here and **Pittston** take you through Scranton's working-class suburbs. Roadside pubs and filling stations abound. Arrive in Pittston and note the town's tagline: Tomato Capital of the World. What must a city do to become tomato capital of the world? For starters, host an annual summer Tomato Festival complete with a Little Miss Tomato competition and a tomato fight at a waterfront parking lot in front of **Cooper's** seafood restaurant. Aside from being great fun, the annual Tomato Festival is a great way to show off the region's high-quality Italian red-sauce cooking, which dates back to the Industrial Revolution and the thousands of Italian immigrants who settled here to work in the mines.

By the 1930s, Pittston-area miners dug up 4 million tons of anthracite a year. City factories produced stoves, electrical equipment, and other finished products. Like other northeastern Pennsylvania coal towns, Pittston has had to cope with a dwindling industrial base. Though empty storefronts dot Main Street, there are also signs of robust civil society. The city's location on the Susquehanna River allows for waterside strolls along the sculpture-lined walkway of River Park. This recreational stretch runs under Fire Fighters' Memorial Bridge, named as a tribute to Pittston firefighters who passed away during a 1993 blaze.

Drive over the Susquehanna and through **West Pittston.** A longtime rival with its neighbor across the river, West Pittston served as a white-collar enclave for manufacturing executives in the Wyoming Valley. As you proceed down US 11 through **Exeter,** note the numerous pizzerias, most of which make great choices for lunch or dinner. I'm partial to **Sabatini's,** where they've been serving up homemade Italian Wedding Soup and thin-crust pizzas with high-quality mozzarella and a semisweet red sauce since 1958.

You might want to work off the pizza, so allow time for a little side trip. Look for the brown sign indicating **Frances Slocum State Park** and make a right onto Eighth Street just outside Exeter. Follow this for 3 miles, and then take a left onto Mount Olivet Road. Drive another mile past Mount Olivet Cemetery and turn into the state park. This is a thousand-acre site, great for amateur hikers and a fine place for a summer picnic. Frances Slocum Lake hosts boaters and bass fishers in the summer and can be used for ice skating in the winter when conditions allow.

Return to US 11 and turn right through the town of **Wyoming** and into **Forty Fort**—named for the 40 New England settlers who planted their roots in the Wyoming Valley when it was a swampy, unprotected swath of northeastern Pennsylvania. There's some notable Revolutionary War history along this route. A thousand British, Loyalist, and Native American sol-

Fire Fighters' Memorial Bridge over the Susquehanna

diers attacked an outmatched group of colonists in what became the Battle of Wyoming on July 3, 1778. It was a terrible defeat, often labeled a massacre or slaughter in the historical literature. The battle did bring some fame to Col. Nathan Denison, one of the 40 original white settlers, who negotiated the colonists' surrender. It's hard to miss the monument to the Battle of Wyoming on the opposite side of US 11. Easier to miss is the rather conventional-looking **Nathan Denison House,** which is a quick right onto Dennison Street off the main drag. The house is historically significant; its original wing (completed in 1790) was joined by a Victorian addition decades later.

Continuing along, find **Plymouth**—a popular community for anthracite families that once was home to two and a half times the number of coal miners that reside throughout the entire region today. Plymouth is a little rougher around the edges than Wyoming or Forty Fort; residential cave-ins were once an all-too-common occurrence around here due to an overabundance of mine tunnels running underground. The route merges with PA 29, and this portion of the drive is peppered with diners and barbecue joints. Try **Stookey's Famous Bar-B-Que,** a couple miles past Plymouth, for tasty sandwiches topped with relish for under four bucks.

Just past Plymouth is the **Susquehanna Riverlands Environmental Preserve and Nature Area.** This well-designed recreational area features a trout-stocked pond and hiking trails rich with birdlife. The clever Planet Walk underscores the expansiveness of the universe—markers along the trail designate all the planets in the solar system (1 foot equals a million miles). Susquehanna Riverlands is operated by the PPL Corporation, which owns and operates a nuclear power plant on the opposite side of US 11. It is hard to miss the massive cooling towers authoritatively fixed into the lush mountain scenery.

Cross into Columbia County and follow the US 11 signs through **Berwick.** If you happen to be here on Thanksgiving, catch the world-famous Run for the Diamonds: a 9-mile loop through Berwick that has been held annually since 1908. The town in those days had a much heavier localized industrial presence, including a large plant operated by American Car and Foundry (ACF), which produced railroad cars here until 1962. The first all-steel coach was produced by ACF in Berwick for the New York City subway. While the factory has left, the central business district remains very much alive, with the nearby power plant and a community hospital serving as employment anchors.

After a stretch of mostly uninteresting furniture stores and car lots, arrive in the meticulously cared-for town of **Bloomsburg.** The incidence of sandwich shops and pizzerias suggests a college presence, and sure enough, nine-thousand-student Bloomsburg University sits atop the northeast section. You don't have to be an undergrad to appreciate the downtown, though, which offers an agreeable diversity of eateries and stores. Bill Hess' Tavern has been packing them in for years (open since 1889), located adjacent to multiple newer bistro-style restaurants. A couple years ago the Prana Juice Bar and Namaste Café opened next door to the venerable Bloomsburg Diner. The café serves a long juice menu and vegetarian delicacies, in its colorful interior and on the large porch overlooking the east end of Bloomsburg's wide Main Street. And the nearby **Inn at Turkey Hill** is an excellent lodging option, with an on-site gourmet dining room frequented by locals.

Switch to PA 42 south just outside Bloomsburg. The route soon bridges the North Branch Susquehanna into **Catawissa,** a small manufacturing town founded by Quakers in 1774. A few stores and taverns are mingled among the residences. The striking redbrick Opera House (tough to miss, with the words *Opera House* painted across the façade in large block letters) punctuates Main Street. Just past here, look for signs indicating a 7-mile side trip to **Knoebels Amusement Resort,** on PA 487 south (the turn occurs at the fork in the road across the street from Tom's Family Restaurant). Cabin rental and campground facilities complement famed Knoebels amusement park, a terrific seasonal attraction that draws families throughout the region from May to September. Highlights include the old wooden roller coasters, vintage bumper cars, a sky ride that vaults up the adjacent mountainside, and the Skloosh water flume, which is a guaranteed soaking for onlookers. It's a great atmosphere and a nice mix of attractions for younger kids and adolescents. Concessions are also a cut above typical amusement-park fare; you can get pierogi (three for two bucks) and tasty potato cakes, as well as fried fish and spaghetti dinners. Admission to Knoebels is free, so pick up ticket books or get a hand stamp for unlimited rides (not available summer weekends). After you're done, return to 42 south and drive through the small farming village of **Numidia.** There is a dragway here, and fresh produce stands are situated outside the town.

The tour concludes with a look at the darker side of coal country. That would be the abandoned town of **Centralia,** which is easy to miss because it no longer really exists. A mine fire has been burning under Centralia since 1962, when an attempt to incinerate the town's landfill inadvertently ignited the anthracite reserves buried beneath. In 1981, after a local boy accidentally plunged through the soil and nearly died, the federal government began paying residents to surrender their property and leave. Eleven years later, this voluntary buyout became an eminent domain taking; the town was deemed uninhabitable due to high levels of toxic gas, and the commonwealth seized and demolished all but a dozen (or so) homes. As of yet, no government entity has found an affordable way to extinguish the fire—cost estimates run well over half a billion dollars—so it continues to burn. Carefully put your hands above the smoking cracks in the soil, and you'll feel the heat rising. The high levels of carbon monoxide and wafting smoke make Centralia the state's most precarious, unique ghost town.

The smoking remains of Centralia

To this day, a few holdouts remain. In June 2009, the state removed a 53-year-old schoolteacher from his home, which was the latest in a long line of takings. Only 10 residents still live in Centralia, nourished by the seclusion, nostalgia, and a belief that the state wants them removed to mine their anthracite.

In *Ghost Towns of Pennsylvania*, Susan Hutchinson Tassin writes, "With all due respect to the few intrepid souls who remain in their homes today, Centralia often looks like a vision of hell, with crumbling infrastructure, silent streets and smoke and sulfurous fumes rising from numerous fissures in the ground throughout the area." Walking around the smoking rubble, it's not hard to see what she's getting at. On the other hand, Centralia is tucked between two perfectly pleasant little towns (**Aristes** and Ashland) and crests into a nice overlook. The steep ups and downs make autumn views from the area's highest points rather beautiful. One can appreciate why so many Centralia residents stayed so long, even as their town smoldered beneath them.

Road signs along PA 42 still list Centralia, but there are no town markers other than a homemade sign reading FIRE that hangs from a gnarled roadside tree and points travelers towards the rubble. At around this area, you may see fellow adventurers pulling off PA 42 past the pits of rubbish and onto the splintered roads that once served a three-thousand-person town. If you visit, exercise caution and watch your step. The route ends near Centralia where it becomes PA 61. You may wish to continue on 61 south to **Ashland,** another 2 miles down the road, and rejoin civilization. The town's **Pioneer Tunnel Coal Mine and Steam Train** offers an edifying tour through an old anthracite mine. Visitors are whisked through in mine cars and learn the finer points of coal mining along the way.

IN THE AREA

Accommodations

Inn at Turkey Hill, 991 Central Road, Bloomsburg. Call 570-387-1500. This wonderful 23-room inn achieves an impressive seclusion considering its proximity to I-80. Rooms are spread throughout three buildings and accommodate a range of budgets. The full breakfast can be taken outside and includes assorted pastries, fruit, and a choice of hot entrée. Web site: www.innatturkeyhill.com.

Radisson Lackawanna Station Hotel Scranton, 700 Lackawanna Road, Scranton. Call 800-395-7046. A converted railroad station distinguished by its grand neoclassical façade is home to six stories of hotel rooms. The renovations are most impressive in the lobby space, which is wrapped in Siena marble. Web site: www.radisson.com/scrantonpa.

Attractions and Recreation

Anthracite Heritage Museum, 159 Cedar Avenue, Scranton. Call 570-963-4804. Open daily, year-round. Web site: www.anthracitemuseum.org.

Archbald Pothole State Park. Call 570-945-3239. Web site: www.dcnr .state.pa.us/stateparks/parks/archbaldpothole.aspx.

Circle Drive In, 1911 Scranton-Carbondale Highway, Dickson City. Call 570-489-5731. Web site: www.circledrivein.com.

Electric City Trolley Museum, 300 Cliff Street, Scranton. Call 570-963-6590. Open daily, Apr.–Dec.; Wed.–Sun., Jan.–Mar. Web site: www.ectma .org.

Frances Slocum State Park, 565 Mount Olivet Road, Wyoming. Call 570-696-3525. Web site: www.dcnr.state.pa.us/stateparks/parks/frances slocum.aspx.

Houdini Museum, 1433 N. Main Avenue, Scranton. Call 570-342-5555. Web site: www.houdini.org.

Knoebels Amusement Resort, Route 487, Elysburg. Call 570-672-9555. Open daily, May–Sept.; weekends only at the beginning and end of the operating season. Call ahead to confirm. Web site: www.knoebels.com.

Mall at Steamtown, 300 The Mall at Steamtown, Scranton. Call 570-343-3400. Web site: www.themallatsteamtown.com.

Nathan Denison House, 35 Denison Street, Forty Fort. Call 570-288-5531.

Pioneer Tunnel Coal Mine and Steam Train, 19th and Oak streets, Ashland. Call 570-875-3850. Open daily, Apr.–Oct.; call ahead to confirm mine tour times. Web site: www.pioneertunnel.com.

Steamtown National Historic Site, Cliff Street, Scranton. Call 570-340-5200. Open daily, year-round. Web site: www.nps.gov/stea.

Susquehanna Riverlands Environmental Preserve and Nature Area, 634 Salem Boulevard, Berwick. Call 866-832-3312. Web site: www.pplweb.com/susquehanna+riverlands.

Wayne County Historical Society, 810 Main Street, Honesdale. Call 570-253-3240. Open Wed.–Sat., Apr.–Dec. Open some Sun. as well. Web site: www.waynehistorypa.org.

Dining and Nightlife

Carmen's Restaurant and Wine Bar, 700 Lackawanna Avenue, Scranton. Call 570-558-3929. Offers quality Italian food at the downtown Scranton Radisson, and a fine Sun. brunch that includes made-to-order omelets, freshly carved meats, and other delicacies served in the unique hotel lobby beneath a Tiffany barrel-vaulted stained-glass ceiling. Open for breakfast, lunch, dinner, and Sun. brunch. Web site: www.carmens radisson.com.

Cooper's on the Waterfront, 304 Kennedy Boulevard, Pittston. Call 570-654-6883. Overlooking the Susquehanna from Pittston, this second branch of the popular Scranton seafood house offers thick crab bisque and Brazilian rock lobster tails, served either indoors or outside by the tiki bar on the Cooper's Cabana deck. Open for lunch, dinner, and late night. Web site: www.coopers-seafood.com.

Sabatini's, 634 Salem Boulevard, Berwick. Call 866-832-3312. Web site: www.pplweb.com/susquehanna+riverlands.

Stookey's Famous Bar-B-Que, 122 E. Poplar Street, Nanticoke. Call 570-735-2162. Terrific roadside sandwich shop. Open for lunch and dinner.

Thai Rak Thai, 349 Adams Avenue, Scranton. Call 570-344-2240. A festive dining room and consistently solid Thai food at this downtown location. Open for lunch and dinner. Web site: www.thairakthaiusa.com.

Other Contacts

Lackawanna County Convention and Visitors Bureau, 99 Glenmaura National Boulevard, Scranton. Call 570-963-6363. Web site: www.visit nepa.org.

Lackawanna Heritage Valley Authority, 538 Spruce Street, Suite 516, Scranton. Call 570-963-6730. Web site: www.lhva.org.

Ricketts Glen State Park

CHAPTER

4

Ricketts Glen and the Endless Mountains

Estimated length: 90 miles
Estimated time: 1–2 days

Getting there: Start in Ricketts Glen State Park, and follow PA 118 east. Turn onto PA 29 north, and take it all the way across the Susquehanna River into Tunkhannock. From here, travel west on US 6 through the Endless Mountains. This drive terminates in Wellsboro.

Highlights: A high-wire drive across the Endless Mountains plateau, this route stretches from the stunning cascades at Ricketts Glen through a popular vacation region known for its clean country air and scenic views. US 6 is a straight shot from Tunkhannock to Wellsboro, midway across the state.

Among the most attractive parts of Pennsylvania, the Endless Mountains attract visitors year-round, especially during leaf-changing season in the fall. US 6 is best seen as a leisurely tour of country scenery, a chance to catch some local culture at the small-town diners and an opportunity to peruse the art galleries or taste local wine. This segment—a little less than half the route across the state's northern tier—is a rich cornucopia of villages and vistas.

The drive begins in **Ricketts Glen State Park,** a perennial candidate for Pennsylvania's most stunning recreational area. Perched atop Red Rock

Mountain, the 13,000-acre park spans three counties. You can arrive here via PA 118 or PA 487. The roads meet near the southeast corner of the park, where you'll find a convenience store and a sportsman's shop. Take 487 north from the intersection of the two roads (a 0.5-mile elevation at its peak) and turn right into the park entrance near Lake Jean. This is where most Ricketts Glen visitors begin their journey, and for good reason.

People come to Ricketts Glen mainly for the waterfalls—there are two dozen to see, and they range in height from the towering Ganoga (94 feet high) to the 15-foot Onondaga. You can hit them all by hiking Falls Trail, which is the park's main attraction. This steep route takes you up, down, over, and around the park's glens and towering hemlock trees, alternating between dirt paths and stone steps. Wooden bridges take hikers over the streams at several points, allowing you to experience the falls from all angles. It's a 7-mile loop total, but you can do 2 or 3 of those miles and still absorb a great deal of natural beauty. Each waterfall somehow has its own personality; you'll pass thundering white-water cascades followed by deliberate, multitiered falls that slither around the rock formations of their glen and drop gently, a few feet at a time.

Signs at the Falls Trail entrances warn of steep and difficult sections. It certainly has its moments. Be methodical, particularly in the early spring when ice sheets tend to linger on flat rocks and make the winding steps downright treacherous. Still, the real danger is less any particular ledge and more the potential for exhaustion. Going down Falls Trail is exhilarating, but coming back up feels like climbing the Empire State Building after donating blood. From bottom to top, the trail is more than a thousand feet high. Wear comfortable hiking gear and be sure to pack sufficient food and water.

Of course, the falls are only the beginning of Ricketts Glen. There is Lake Jean, where you can fish for bass, picnic by the shore, or rent a rowboat. And while the Falls Trail cannot be biked (you'd be crazy to try anyway), several biking trails can be found in the park's northernmost section. There are other, flatter hiking trails around here, too.

It is unconventional to start a scenic drive at a state park; most routes in this book begin in larger towns with at least a few lodging options in the immediate area. The closest towns around Ricketts Glen are tiny, but you've got some options. The park itself boasts a 120-site campground, as well as 10 very nice cabins, all of which are highly convenient to Falls Trail. These can be rented by the week during the summer (between $300 and $500 depending on size and residency—Pennsylvanians get a price break) or for shorter stays in the autumn, winter, and spring. And conveniently located just outside the park's PA 118 entrance point is the six room **Ricketts Glen Hotel.**

Once you're done with Ricketts Glen, proceed east along PA 118. Pass the Trail's End Restaurant, a 10-table (plus counter) diner featuring lunch and dinner specials for under 10 dollars a plate. The Trail's End has been feeding hungry hikers for more than 30 years. There is not much else along the 10 miles between Ricketts Glen and PA 29, but you may wish to stop at the Mountain View Barn to browse country antiques.

Turn left onto PA 29 north at the Shell station in the small town of **Pikes Creek.** Pass Joe's Christmas Tree Farm and continue left along PA 29 when the road hits PA 415. From here it's 3 short miles to the old lumbering village of **Noxen,** which is stringed with residences, churches, farming equipment, and a food mart. This segment of the route dances around Bowman's Creek at several points. The creek is an interesting waterway—slim relative to the nearby Susquehanna, it nevertheless pulls together tributaries from the Luzerne County mountain region and is popular with fly fishermen. The creek is rich with trout during the spring, and there are plenty of suitable spots along PA 29 where you can stop to cast a rod if the mood strikes.

Stay left on PA 29 where the route hits the 309 junction. Swing past the flashy Fireplace Gallery and descend through an intersection with PA 292. The route flattens out a little here, continuing over Bowman's Creek again and past Marsha's Sugar Hollow Diner. You'll find yourself greeted by the gateway to two-thousand-person **Tunkhannock:** a small airport, a Wal-mart, a shopping center, and the mammoth North Branch of the Susquehanna River.

Tunkhannock is a fine town. Like many in the region, it owes its existence to the lumber industry, which boomed in the mid-19th century. Its Native American name means (among other things) "full of timber." A few remnants of the lumber era remain today, including the Prince Hotel and Red Lion Inn restaurant, which opened in 1844 as Wall's Hotel. The place is showing its age, but you can still have a drink and a cigarette in the bar area, where the stained-glass windows and pool table summon a different era. The food is all right; other options are **Twigs Café** (cozy) or **Seasons** restaurant (BYOB), both of which serve excellent contemporary fare. All these properties are found along Tioga Street, which is the main downtown business strip. There are a couple interesting variety stores and boutique shops here as well. Another Tunkhannock highlight is the **Die-**

Wyalusing Hotel, the social hub of a small town

trich Theater. Built in 1936 and renovated in 2001, the Dietrich screens first-run movie releases and hosts theatrical productions. A small gallery space in the hallway entrance and an art studio round out the offerings that make the Dietrich a bona fide cultural center.

Tunkhannock also marks another contact with US 6, the famous scenic route that spans the entire length of northern Pennsylvania. The route is known alternately as the Grand Army of the Republic Highway and actually stretches from ocean to ocean. But the Pennsylvania segment is the most celebrated piece, connecting picturesque small towns across scenic mountain terrain and offering travelers several reasons to stop: vineyards, art galleries, restaurants, recreation, and shopping curiosities. The route has its own tourist association and its own Web site. It doubles as a state bike route

(Route Y), so keep a lookout for cyclists whizzing along the shoulder. For part of this particular drive, US 6 runs alongside the Susquehanna River. The next drive follows US 6 all the way to the Allegheny National Forest.

As you cross the Susquehanna into Tunkhannock, skip past US 6 to Business US 6 west and tour downtown. The business route joins the main US 6 near the Tunkhannock Public Library, where the road twists into the mountains and alternates between two and three lanes. You'll soon hit **Meshoppen,** a small farming town, and the Wyoming County Fairgrounds. There are a few motels and campgrounds around Meshoppen in case you wish to stop for the night.

Eight miles past Meshoppen at the PA 367 junction is **Laceyville.** Just off US 6 sits Laceyville's sleepy little downtown, where you'll find a barber shop, bank, propane store, and the Wiser Choice restaurant, which serves breakfast and lunch daily and dinner Wednesday through Friday. From Laceyville, the route inclines sharply into Bradford County. Beyond the county line is greater **Wyalusing** ("good hunting grounds") and Grovedale Winery and Vineyard, which is across the street from Wyalusing Junior/ Senior High School (just off US 6). A variety of wines are produced here, with a slight emphasis on dry and semidry whites. The tasting room is bright and attractive—a popular place for parties and events or a single leisurely glass.

Another place you can sample Grovedale wines is the restaurant at the 10-room **Wyalusing Hotel.** This beautifully gabled, gingerbread-colored building dates back to 1926 and is the center of civic life in Wyalusing. It's especially popular for brunch and Sunday dinner, a place where you'll find hostesses greeting patrons by name and three cuts of prime rib.

West of Wyalusing, US 6 makes a steep incline that crests into two scenic overlooks separated by 2 miles on the south side of the road. Take a moment to observe the countryside and a bend in the mighty Susquehanna. The second stop is the **Marie Antoinette Scenic Overlook,** which faces the site of the **French Azilum.** Few have ever heard of this place, but it's an interesting story. After the French Revolution, a group of loyalists fled to America and took up residence at this planned community in Bradford County (*azilum* is French for *asylum*), which was underwritten by American financiers like the already expatriated Stephen Girard. Legend has it that Marie Antoinette herself planned on escaping to the Azilum had she avoided the guillotine. The settlement was dissolved a decade after its founding; it never really took off, and Napoleon allowed settlers to return

home in 1803. You can visit the site itself—now a state-sponsored historical attraction with an admission charge—farther along the route. A gateway to the French Azilum is the town of **Wysox,** where US 6 meets PA 187.
It's an 8-mile side trip along PA 187 south and a couple other back roads,
but signage is excellent, and the route is attractive. When you arrive at the
Azilum, you'll find several reconstructed log houses similar to the ones
inhabited by the French royalists (sadly, no original structures remain).
There's also a labyrinth, nature trail, and picnic area, all of which are accessible May through October.

Wysox has a couple stores and an ice cream stand, but there's much
more across the river in **Towanda.** The town slopes up steeply from the
west bank of the Susquehanna where a paved walking path hugs the river.
An impressive architectural stock offers some clues of Towanda's history—the town hooked into the region's expansive canal system and thrived
as a mid-19th-century hub for textiles and lumber. The manufacturing
brought significant wealth to Towanda, and the boom lasted through the
early 20th century, overlapping a sterling era for American architecture.
Several remarkable buildings emerged. Check out the **Keystone Theatre,**

Reconstructed French Azilum structure

a stunning Romanesque structure that still bears the nameplate of Hale's Opera House, which it was called when it opened in 1887. The Keystone features both live performances and film screenings. Also worth a look are the beaux-arts county courthouse and the nifty little historical society and museum that occupy the former county jail. For food, Towanda has two colorful diners: the transplanted and restored Red Rose Diner or **Cookie's Canteen,** which doubles as a gift shop.

A visit to the local branch of Ben Franklin Crafts on the cusp of downtown took me on a walk down memory lane—you don't see variety stores like this much anymore. What would once have been called a five and dime, Ben Franklin sells everything from model car kits to paintbrushes and greeting cards. As you leave Towanda and enter North Towanda Township, note the elaborate Queen Anne mansions along the roadside—these belonged to financiers and manufacturing executives who formed the region's upper class in the industrial era. A few properties have been converted to lavish bed & breakfasts, like the Victorian Charm Inn. Though Towanda's days as a manufacturing hub have gone the way of the canal as a transportation network, it remains a robust small town (partly thanks to US 6 tourism) and is well worth exploring. If you missed lunchtime in Towanda, stop a few miles outside town at **Le Roy's Gourmet Subs & Pizza.**

Pass the PA 220 intersection and continue to **Luthers Mills.** For a brief adventure, follow the weather-beaten signs a mile off the main road to the **Luther's Mill covered bridge.** As visitors to Bucks County and greater Lancaster know, Pennsylvania is rich with these unique bridges, but this is the last remaining one in Bradford.

Drive slowly along the gravel roads back from the bridge, return to US 6 west, and travel through **Burlington** and past its active quarry. A couple miles off the road (a winding, uphill trip) is another worthwhile diversion— **Mount Pisgah State Park.** An environmental interpretive center and a 75-acre fishing and boating lake are highlights. Hunters track deer and rabbit in the bordering game land. Drive around this area a while, and you'll probably spot trucks transporting heavy machinery; odds are you're spitting distance from a natural gas well. Bradford and neighboring Tioga County are home to substantial gas reserves and a number of the state's Marcellus shale wells. (For more on the natural-gas drilling phenomenon that has swept rural Pennsylvania, see chapter 9.)

The next town is **Troy,** which proudly underscores the region's agricultural traditions. A mile east of downtown is the **Troy Farm Museum,** requiring a short trip along PA 14. The museum is a comprehensive collection of farm tools and machinery; it sits inside Alparon Park and the local fairgrounds, which are active most spring and summer weekends with horse shows, shooting competitions, and other events. The annual Troy Fair takes place in late July. Downtown Troy is smaller and less architecturally imposing than Towanda, but it's dotted with luncheonettes and small stores.

Traveling west, Troy gives way to sparsely populated **Sylvania** borough. Stop at County Sampler Antiques—a rare rural Pennsylvania antiques shop open seven days a week—that features all sorts of Americana from several local dealers. Then cross the county line into Tioga—less populated and a bit more spread out than its neighbor to the east. US 6 twists and turns past dairy farms, horse farms, and cattle farms, as well as adapted green space like Corey Creek Golf Club, and eventually meanders into **Mansfield.** The gateway is 3,400-student Mansfield University, a former teachers college.

Since it's a college town, Mansfield has a different feel than the surrounding area. Yes, there are the usual antiques stores, but also funky coffeehouses like the celestially decorated **Night and Day Coffee Café,** which was founded by a Mansfield University grad. The restaurant scene is a little more interesting, too. The **Wren's Nest** (just outside downtown) is one nice choice—contemporary Continental fare and occasional Wednesday jazz nights are the highlights.

If you're in the mood for one final diversion before the drive wraps up, follow the slightly confusing signs 5 miles off US 6 to **Hills Creek State Park.** Due in part to the popularity of nearby Pine Creek Gorge (see chapter 5) and its small size, Hills Creek is a little undervisited. Its remote location makes it a haven for all sorts of wildlife, including a beaver settlement. The warm-water lake is open from Memorial Day to Labor Day for fishing and swimming. Ten cabins are an affordable alternative to the hotels of nearby **Wellsboro,** where the drive terminates. These other lodging options include the nicely maintained **Sherwood Motel** and the 140-year-old **Penn Wells.** If visiting the latter, check out the American flag on display in the lobby, which is assembled entirely from glass ornaments. This is a nod to the regional glass industry—especially robust on the New York side of the nearby New York–Pennsylvania border, where glass manufacturer Corning is based.

Everyone loves Wellsboro, blessed with a perfect location in the heart of north-central Pennsylvania. Its lively gaslit Main Street, shoebox-sized diner, and renovated **Arcadia movie theater** make it a popular stop on US

Luther's Mill covered bridge, slightly hidden off US 6

6 for everyone from retirees to Mansfield students. There's some restaurant variety here, including Italian flavors at Timeless Destination and serviceable Chinese food at Dumpling House. Wellsboro enjoys a brisk tourist season from April to November—it is the closest major town to Pine Creek Gorge, known more famously as Pennsylvania's Grand Canyon, covered at length in the next drive.

IN THE AREA

Accommodations
US 6 has plenty of inns and motels, but lodging options around Ricketts Glen are more limited. For those who can't live without the creature comforts of a national hotel chain or posh bed & breakfast, Wilkes-Barre and

Bloomsburg are within a half-hour drive and offer several hotels. You can also find a few private campgrounds within 10 miles of the park.

Penn Wells, 62 Main Street, Wellsboro. Call 570-724-2111. Web site: www.pennwells.com.

Ricketts Glen Hotel, 221 PA 118, Benton. Call 570-477-3656. Just outside the park on PA 118, this hotel has six rooms and a rustic bar/restaurant. Web site: www.rickettsglenhotel.net.

Sherwood Motel, 2 Main Street, Wellsboro. Call 570-724-3424. A simple but well-cared-for 42-room motel conveniently located in downtown Wellsboro. The heated outdoor pool is a nice amenity. Web site: www .sherwoodmotel.org.

Wyalusing Hotel, 111 Main Street, Wyalusing. Call 570-746-1204. This renovated property dominates the Wyalusing streetscape with its colorful façade and second-story Mississippi riverboat porch. After hours, the attached country barn bar hums until 2 AM on weekends. Web site: www .wyalusinghotel.org.

Attractions and Recreation

Arcadia Theatre, 50 Main Street, Wellsboro. Call 570-724-4957. Web site: www.arcadiawellsboro.com.

Dietrich Theater, 60 E. Tioga Street, Tunkhannock. Call 570-836-1022. Web site: www.dietrichtheater.com.

French Azilum, Route 456, near Towanda. Call 570-265-3376. Web site: www.frenchazilum.com.

Hills Creek State Park, 32–36 Central Avenue, Wellsboro. Call 570-724-4246. Web site: www.dcnr.state.pa.us/stateparks/parks/hillscreek.aspx.

Keystone Theatre, 601 Main Street, Towanda. Call 570-268-2787. Web site: www.bcrac.org.

Mount Pisgah State Park, Troy. Call 570-297-2734. Web site: www.dcnr .state.pa.us/stateparks/parks/mtpisgah.aspx.

Ricketts Glen State Park, 695 State Route 487, Benton. Call 570-477-5675. Web site: www.dcnr.state.pa.us/stateparks/parks/rickettsglen.aspx.

Troy Farm Museum, US 6 and PA 14, Troy. Call 570-297-3410. Open Thurs.–Sun., May–Oct. Web site: www.troyfarmmuseum.org.

Dining and Nightlife

Cookie's Canteen, 318 Main Street, Towanda. Call 570-265-2488. An extraordinarily extensive breakfast menu is served all day at this friendly Towanda diner and gift shop. Open for breakfast and lunch. Web site: www.cookiescanteen.com.

Le Roy's Gourmet Subs & Pizza, US 6, Towanda. Call 570-265-9322. The outdoor deck looks out on farmland and the Appalachians, and the oversized sub sandwiches and wings are pretty good. NASCAR paraphernalia covers the walls.

Night and Day Coffee Café, 2 N. Main Street, Mansfield. Hip, friendly coffee shop serving excellent coffee and sweet treats. Web site: www.night anddaycoffee.com.

Seasons, 53 E. Tioga Street, Tunkhannock. Call 570-836-3080. Open for lunch and dinner. Web site: www.seasonsdowntowne.com.

Twigs Restaurant and Café, 1 E. Tioga Street, Tunkhannock. Call 570-836-0433. Good burgers, sandwiches, and seafood served in a colorful dining room. Casual. Open for lunch and dinner. Web site: www.twigs cafe.com.

Wren's Nest, 102 W. Wellsboro Street, Mansfield. Call 570-662-1093. Open for lunch and dinner. Web site: www.wrensnestpa.com.

Other Contacts

Endless Mountains Visitors Bureau, 4 Werks Plaza, US 6, Tunkhannock. Call 570-836-5431. Web site: www.endlessmountains.org.

Pennsylvania Route 6 Tourist Association. Call 814-435-7706. Web site: www.paroute6.com.

North-Central Pennsylvania is lumber country.

CHAPTER

5

Lumbering Across the Northern Tier

Estimated length: 90 miles
Estimated time: 1–2 days

Getting there: Start in Wellsboro and follow PA 660 west to Leon Harrison State Park. Loop back around after touring the East Rim of Pine Creek Gorge and follow back to US 6, exploring as much of the West Rim and the Pine Creek Trail as time allows. Continue west on US 6 through to Smethport.

Highlights: A more rustic segment than the previous tour, this drive showcases Pennsylvania's proud lumbering heritage and travels through thinly populated towns recessed deep into the north-central and northwest region like Galeton and Coudersport. It begins near Pennsylvania's Grand Canyon.

Northern Pennsylvania might seem like a hodgepodge of charming small towns linked by a scenic byway. In fact, there is an economic and cultural coherence to the region that explains its quirks. The previous drive covered a portion of the eastern leg of US 6, where farming and light manufacturing predominated through the early 20th century. Access to arable land and the North Branch of the Susquehanna made this possible. As one travels west, the towns grow farther apart, and the open spaces grow

Black Hawaiian sheep congregate at Animaland.

increasingly vast. Tioga County has 20,000 fewer residents than Bradford County, its neighbor to the east. Potter County, next down the line, has fewer still. Changes are subtle at first but easy to see if you're looking. Gun clubs and sportsmen's shops replace dairy farms and wineries. Bumper stickers trumpet gun rights, and snowmobiles speed through the parks. All-terrain vehicles materialize roadside as abruptly as the white-tailed deer. It's been hundreds of years since European settlers arrived in this densely wooded mountain region, but a frontier mentality pervades.

This drive begins in Wellsboro, where the last drive left off. The town brands itself as the gateway to Pennsylvania's Grand Canyon—a reference to dazzling Pine Creek Gorge, which is about 10 miles south and west of town. If you plan on lingering around the canyon (you can fill a half day easily, more if you try) visit the **Tioga County Visitors Bureau** for maps and suggestions. Then head west on PA 660, a tricky little road with several sudden turns.

Between Wellsboro and the canyon are a couple notables. The **Animaland Zoological Park** features more than two dozen species in a small, 12-acre facility on the edge of a sharp PA 660 right turn. Pygmy goats, Black Hawaiian sheep, and a pair of emus are among the more exotic creatures. Feed them dried corn and Fruit Loops through the fences; they've been well conditioned to expect food from visitors and gravitate toward the sound of tourists' footsteps. A few animals get free rein, so you may see some uncaged ducks hanging around. But a heavy-duty fence is the closest you'll get to a North American black bear unless you unwisely leave leftovers by a campsite in Allegheny National Forest.

Next door to Animaland is the Grand Canyon Motel & Resort, with a rustic bar and billiards area. If you're curious, drive up the inclined road past the motel, following the signs that read TOWER. This will take you past a campground and all the way to a hundred-foot-tall steel observation tower. Swipe a credit card through the turnstile machine ($3) and wait for the robot voice to authorize entry. Walk the eight flights of stairs and take in the panoramic views, which are 2,100 feet above sea level. It's a nice little diversion, but to be truthful, a few miles along the route are even better views for free.

PA 660 culminates in **Leonard Harrison State Park,** which is the eastern rim of the Grand Canyon. The overlook from here is simply incredible. Seventeen hundred feet below is the canyon itself, where Pine Creek whisks ant-sized kayakers downstream and ant-sized cars stop roadside to appreciate the enormity of the mountains. Watch for turkey vultures, ospreys, and even the occasional bald eagle from the overlook areas. These birds soar high over the canyon, doing reconnaissance for food and nesting real estate.

Two hiking trails originate from the east rim. Turkey Path is the big one—a mile long in each direction, this trail takes you all the way down to the creek. Hiking Turkey Path is as exhausting as hiking Ricketts Glen (origination point for the previous drive), but the route is well blazed and worth the views if you have the energy. A less difficult, though somewhat

The breathtaking Pennsylvania Grand Canyon

challenging hike is the Overlook Trail, which loops around the east rim but doesn't go too far down toward the gorge. Keep in mind that Turkey Path is only open seasonally, from the first weekend in April to November. But you can catch views of the canyon year-round.

When you're done with the east rim, spin the car around and head back along PA 660 east. At the white church where 660 meets State Road 3029, turn left onto the state road for less than a mile. Pass the regional airport, and then make another left onto PA 362. This will deposit you at the bottom of the canyon and Pine Creek. Parallel to the water is the paved Pine Creek Rail Trail. This is one of several Rails to Trails biking and jogging paths in Pennsylvania, and it runs 59 miles from the canyon area down to Jersey Shore in Lycoming County. It's a great bike ride. Another option is to contact the **Mountain Trail Horse Center** and take a covered wagon ride down along a portion of the creek.

PA 362 hits US 6 at **Ansonia.** Make a left here, and then another very quick left onto Forest Road (basically a U-turn around the tavern), and then drive across the creek and up toward the west rim of the Grand Canyon, known as **Colton Point State Park.** Colton Point gets a bit less tourist traffic than the east rim, but the drive up is just as elevated, and the view of the gorge is just as good. There are two separate hiking trails that, like Turkey Path, send you down to Pine Creek. Stay away from the privately owned cabins on this side; if you wish to spend the night, the campsites at Colton Point are quite nice. Return to US 6 by turning back when you've had your fill of the west rim.

Somewhere between Tioga and Potter counties, take a mental inventory of what you've seen so far, and it will occur to you that mostly you've seen trees. And then more trees. Timber occupies the majority of all land in north-central Pennsylvania, just as it did when European settlers arrived here more than three hundred years ago. But a lot of things happened between then and now.

When the first streams of colonists arrived on the eastern shores of the New World, most settled near the coast. They began planting crops and building cities, moving inland gradually and establishing agrarian villages along the way. Access to water and farmable land were the main prerequisites for most settlers, which is why the vast majority stopped when they hit the Alleghenies. But a handful made the unconventional decision to live their lives in the mountains. They were early American iconoclasts, choosing isolation and adventure in the woods over anything else the new country had to offer. Subsistence ruled their lives. And since not much grew in the mountains besides pine and hemlock trees, logging occupied virtually all their time. Hunting occupied the rest.

The difficulty of surviving in the mountains kept the population extraordinarily low. It was not until the early 19th century that anyone began paying attention to Pennsylvania timber and the people who logged it. A population boom in East Coast cities and rural New England created overwhelming demand for raw materials, including lumber. The nascent industry gained relevance in the 1820s. Potter County contained fewer than two hundred people, but that was enough to form a couple earnest small towns. Entrepreneurs set up water-powered saw mills and floated their logs downriver to industrial hubs in central Pennsylvania like Williamsport, Emporium, and Lock Haven. As America grew and the need for lumber expanded, new waves of settlers found their way to the Pennsylvania Wilds. The first major commercial lumber outfit was formed in 1840.

The next 40 years brought consistent growth to the region. Small towns like Galeton, Ulysses, Gaines, and the Potter County seat of Coudersport mushroomed. School systems were formed and hotels erected. Immigrants helped fill out the countryside—a small German enclave (Germania) was settled in 1855. Norwegian violinist Ole Bull attempted, unsuccessfully, to establish a Norwegian logging and farming town south of Galeton. And large numbers of Italian loggers planted roots in the region, particularly after the Civil War. Eventually, the immigrants were followed by the railroads—a double edged sword that ultimately doomed timber country for a generation.

Train service was extended to north-central Pennsylvania in the 1880s, and the logging industry expanded at a feverish pace. In a matter of decades the north-central Pennsylvania forests were stripped bare. The lumber companies were unbothered—they had access to the entire continental United States, which was still full of virgin timber. All they had to do was send the trains somewhere else. By 1920, the north-central forest region was little more than pine stumps. Lumber towns that had failed to diversify their economies hemorrhaged population.

In some ways, those who remained in the north-central Pennsylvania forests through the 1920s and the Great Depression resembled the isolated adventurers who occupied this territory during the original European settlement. The WPA *Guide to Pennsylvania,* published in 1940, has a revealing snippet about those who chose to live there at the time: "In this wild and remote region, devastated by forest fires and reckless lumbering, dwell a people who might be termed the 'Pennsylvania mountaineers.' Their houses are often mere shacks or cabins on small and unproductive farm patches. Meager produce from the soil and the money gained by selling hides and furs provide all the material things they use. They seek no contact with the outside world, and discourage investigation."

But as we are reminded driving along US 6 today, the history does not end there. The reforestation of north-central Pennsylvania is among the state's greatest success stories of the 20th century. The work began under famed governor Gifford Pinchot, who was elected in the early 1920s during the forests' darkest, barest era. A pragmatic environmentalist, Pinchot's reforesting agenda was supplanted by federal investment from President Roosevelt and the Civilian Conservation Corps (also responsible for developing many state parks and recreational facilities mentioned in this book). It took a substantial commitment and decades of work, but second-generation hardwood forests now blanket north-central Pennsylvania. The logging industry today is more specialized and genuinely sustainable. Population in these north-central lumber towns receded significantly after the boom but has stabilized since. Artisanal furniture stores and clean country air have replaced the barren, burnt-out wilderness. And throughout Tioga, Potter, and McKean counties—among Pennsylvania's most conservative areas—an environmentalist streak colors the local politics. Longtime residents appreciate the time and effort it took to rebuild these forests, and nobody wants to go back.

For the whole story, stop by the **Pennsylvania Lumber Museum** just past **Galeton.** This is the easternmost town in Potter County, with a 1,200-person population and one of few stoplights you'll see on this segment of US 6 (at the intersection of PA 144). Before the museum, stop in at the Brick House Café and Deli, which is a cozy little spot for coffee and snacks. The hip-roofed brick building is more than a hundred years old and has some nice porch seating overlooking the town. Across the street is the Heart's Desire country shop, housed in an old hardware store. Books, antiques, foodstuffs, and other curiosities are stocked throughout; the most interesting stuff is on the second level.

It's a mostly uneventful ride between Galeton and **Coudersport,** the next major stop along US 6. You'll pass the lumber museum and find skiers, tubers, and snowboarders gathering at Ski Denton (22 trails of varying difficulty), on the opposite side of the road. In the warmer months, mountain bikers navigate Denton Hill's steep incline (2,400 feet above sea level at its highest point). Skiing, hunting, and golfing attract outdoorsmen and recreationalists who frequently spend the night; rustic lodges like the **Potato City Country Inn** line the route from Galeton to Coudersport. The latter offers more in the way of luxury accommodations.

Coudersport (pronounced "Cow-dersport") is a fun little town. Positioned neatly beside a hulking stretch of mountains, where the Allegheny River first bisects US 6, the scenic Potter County seat has drawn tourism for more than a century. In a foregone era, weekenders might have spent the night at the redbrick Coudersport Hotel, where Main Street and Second Street form downtown's central point. Fortunately enough, the property was beautifully restored some 30 years ago and continues on as the **Crittenden Hotel.** Owner Walter Baker can be spotted regularly circulating the hotel's fine restaurant, carving roasts on buffet nights and chatting up guests. His affability is characteristic of Coudersport on the whole. Locals mingle with visitors in and around the business district's attractively preserved Greek Revival buildings. The county courthouse mixes that style with Italianate flourishes added in a Victorian-era remodeling. Nearby is a small arboretum, marked by an old caboose, as well as **Olga's Gallery and Café:** a fun spot to relax over a cup of coffee and browse Ukrainian deco-

---

THE WELL-TRAVELED DAVID ZEISBERGER

Coudersport is one of numerous Pennsylvania towns where you'll encounter a memorial or historical plaque dedicated to David Zeisberger—a Moravian missionary who traversed Pennsylvania for six decades, converting Native Americans to his faith and settling new Moravian communities. Love the mission or loathe the mission, you can't argue with Zeisberger's productivity: a speaker of several Indian languages, his influence extended from the Moravian settlement at Bethlehem in the Lehigh Valley all the way through Ohio. He was among the first Europeans to travel around the north-central region, which is why he is memorialized in Coudersport. You may have also spotted a historic marker to Zeisberger in Wyalusing (see chapter 4), where he successfully converted many Native Americans.

---

rated eggs, among other curiosities. Of course, any small Pennsylvania town this charming comes complete with a beautifully restored 1920s movie theater.

Leaving Coudersport, pass a memorable roadside cemetery and continue west through **Roulette** and then across the McKean County border into **Port Allegany** on the Allegheny River's banks. Once referred to as "Canoe Place" by Native Americans who observed white settlers building and repairing pine canoes near the riverbanks, this is an example of an old lumber town that has adjusted smoothly to the post-lumber-boom era. The transition was made easier by companion industries like natural gas extraction and glass production. The economic backbone of Port Allegany remains the glass industry and its two remaining plants—one operated by the Saint Gobain container corporation and the other by Pittsburgh Corning.

You'll lose the river for a while after Port Allegany, but continue through McKean County and finish the drive in **Smethport.** Though somewhat rougher around the edges than comparable Coudersport, this is a pleasant town and well worth exploring. Several Gilded Age mansions survive, most dating back to the era when Smethport financier Henry Hamlin went into business underwriting debt for lumber companies operating in northwestern Pennsylvania. Hamlin's name is featured prominently on local institutions, including Hamlin Lake in the heart of town. There are other notable attractions in Smethport, including the **McKean County Historical Society** and jail museum. Smethport is also the birthplace of the Wooly Willy toy. Don't pretend you don't remember Wooly Willy. Remember manipulating a thin magnet to move the metal grindings around and give the bald guy hair and eyebrows?

IN THE AREA

Accommodations

Potato City Country Inn, 3084 E. Second Street, Coudersport. Call 814-274-8133. This two-story brick lodge is patronized by sportsmen, including ATV enthusiasts, snowmobilers, golfers, hunters, and the skiing set who like the location near Denton Hill. Potato City offers 30 conventional motel rooms as well as three detached, pitched-roof apartments for larger groups. Web site: www.potatocitycountryinn.com.

Attractions and Recreation

Animaland Zoological Park, 4181 Route 660, Wellsboro. Call 570-724-4546. Open daily, May–Oct. Web site: www.animalandzoo.com.

Colton Point State Park, Wellsboro. Call 570-724-3061. Web site: www.dcnr.state.pa.us/stateparks/parks/coltonpoint.aspx.

Leonard Harrison State Park, 4797 Route 660, Wellsboro. Call 570-724-3061. Web site: www.dcnr.state.pa.us/stateparks/parks/leonard harrison.aspx.

McKean County Historical Society, 502 W. King Street, Smethport. Call 814-887-5142. Open Tues. and Thurs., Apr.–Oct., with additional weekdays during July and Aug. Web site: www.smethportchamber.com /old_jail_museum.htm.

Mountain Trail Horse Center, 4755 US 6, Wellsboro. Call 570-723-1645. Web site: www.mountaintrailhorse.com.

Pennsylvania Lumber Museum, 5660 Route 6 W., Galeton. Call 814-435-2652. Open Wed.–Sun., Sept.–Mar. Call to confirm hours. Web site: www.lumbermuseum.org.

Dining and Nightlife

Crittenden Hotel, 133 N. Main Street, Coudersport. Call 814-274-8320. Excellent American food, a cut or two above the quality of the many diners and cafés found along US 6. Look for buffet specials on weekends. Open for lunch and dinner.

Olga's Gallery and Café, 107 E. Second Street, Coudersport. Call 814-274-0794. Web site: www.eggdecorator.com.

Other Contacts

Pennsylvania Route 6 Tourist Association. Call 814-435-7706. Web site: www.paroute6.com.

Tioga County Visitors Bureau, 114 Main Street #4, Wellsboro. Call 570-723-1016. Web site: www.visittiogapa.com.

Kinzua Reservoir at Allegheny National Forest

CHAPTER

6

Great Forests— Part 1

Estimated length: 78 miles
Estimated time: 1 day

Getting there: Continuing from Smethport, travel west on PA 59. Immediately after crossing the James Morrison Memorial Bridge just before the Kinzua Dam, make a left onto Forest Road 262, also known as the Long House Scenic Drive. Follow the scenic byway down to PA 321 south and continue on 321 for 9 miles, where the route merges with US 219. Follow 219 south 15 miles into Ridgway.

Highlights: This ride suggests a trip through the Bradford Ranger District of the Allegheny National Forest, Pennsylvania's only national forest and a living textbook on how to replant a complex ecosystem. The several recreational opportunities along the way include sunning around Kinzua Reservoir and camping at Kiasutha. The tour concludes with a string of mountain towns in the northwest frontier counties.

It took barely 50 years to destroy the Pennsylvania forests. If they had been left as they were in 1920, a mature second growth along the northern tier would still be 30 years away as of this writing. But the hundreds of thousands of acres laden with black cherry, maple, ash, oak, pine, and hemlock that occupy this region today reveal a better history. The forests were carefully rebuilt, thanks to aggressive leadership from a few shrewd public administrators and the advantageous timing of the otherwise hideous Great Depression.

The previous drive referenced Gifford Pinchot and his mission to reforest Pennsylvania. Pinchot is an intriguing historical figure—a moderate Republican in the mold of Teddy Roosevelt, he transformed the government's approach to forestry at both the national and state level. Following in the footsteps of Joseph Rothrock, Pennsylvania's original forester and conservation advocate, Pinchot refined the politics of environmentalism into an influential credo. As a consequence of the country's rapid growth and seemingly limitless territory, few Americans even knew what conservation was prior to the 20th century. As Pinchot introduced the concept into public policy (first at the U.S. Forestry Service and later as a state official), he simultaneously focused his attention on making conservation a productive, profitable tool. Pinchot and his acolytes were not merely interested in returning Pennsylvania forests to their native state. They wanted to make the forests a sustainable economic resource—something that could provide jobs and economic development for the region without the merciless exploitation that characterized the late-19th-century lumber boom.

Thanks to Pinchot, a sustainable lumber economy endures in north-central Pennsylvania. This has required some compromises, including the planting of nonnative but commercially useful second-growth tree varieties (chiefly black cherry). There are also oil pumps and natural gas wells scattered throughout, most noticeably roadside around Allegheny National Forest, where leases to the industry help to pay for maintaining the forest and recreational areas. This is not without controversy. Some environmentalists argue for a complete ban, and the expansion of natural gas drilling in state forests has really heated up as of late (see the chapter 9 sidebar). Others accept a modest industrial presence as an acceptable compromise, so long as the conservation activities endure.

Back in the early 1900s, the situation was much more severe. But overlogging and out-of-control forest fires were not unique to Pennsylvania, and advocates like Pinchot eventually got through to Congress. The Weeks Act, passed in 1911, opened the door for using federal funds to purchase and care for national forests. Ten years later, the Department of Agriculture acquired the **Allegheny National Forest** in northwest Pennsylvania. Its steep plateaus and ravaged appearance made rebuilding a tall order, but the seeds were being planted—both literally and figuratively—for the kind of statewide renewal that Pinchot and Rothrock had been advocating for years.

As he was working his way through the bureaucracies in Washington and Harrisburg, Pinchot developed a close relationship with Franklin Roosevelt—then a New York politician—who was sympathetic to Pinchot's environmental agenda. When his own political career took off in 1922, newly minted Governor Pinchot continued acquiring decimated woodlands and beginning the arduous reforestation process with the resources available, a project he saw through until six years later when the stock market crashed and the bottom fell out on the American economy. Roosevelt's election as president in 1932 opened the door for creative new public spending programs to put Americans back to work. A signature New Deal effort, Roosevelt's Civilian Conservation Corps (CCC) sought to merge remaking rural America with reemploying the out-of-work millions. Dreamed up by Roosevelt shortly after his inauguration, it would become the least controversial, most universally beloved New Deal program and the key to rebuilding the Pennsylvania forests.

For Pinchot and Pennsylvania, the timing was ideal. As Joseph Speakman notes in *At Work in Penn's Woods: The Civilian Conservation Corps in Pennsylvania,* the Keystone State was uniquely positioned to benefit from a program like the CCC. Regenerating the northern tier forests was a truly massive undertaking, but the state's well-managed forest service had already begun the work and was prepared to expand its scope. All that was needed were volunteers; unlike sparsely populated western and plains states where public works projects also demanded substantial man hours, Pennsylvania had both a large population and among the highest unemployment rates in the country. The Great Depression hit the rural boomtowns and resource-starved countryside as hard as it hit Philadelphia and Pittsburgh. This provided the CCC with an unusually diverse labor pool from which to draw. Pennsylvania's CCC camps were flooded with applications from the onset and brought together a diverse cross section of Pennsylvania men (unfortunately, this diversity did not extend to race—CCC camps, like most of the era's public works programs, were racially segregated).

The first CCC camp in Pennsylvania was in the Allegheny National Forest. ANF-1/Company 318, as it was known, was the second camp in the whole country. Its men planted more than a million trees by 1935, and the 13 ANF camps that followed were similarly productive. Tree planting was just the beginning—CCC camps in the Allegheny National Forest erected telephone poles, laid hiking trails, built cabins and roads, and made countless other improvements that created the modern ANF. The forest's half million acres (a quarter of the state's government-owned land) were transformed from barren, burnt-out nothingness into the thickly wooded recreational Shangri-la it is today. With two ranger districts including more than 200 miles of hiking trails, two picturesque rivers, assorted camping and boating opportunities, and a 96-mile shoreline set against a 12,000-acre reservoir, the forest's size can make it overwhelming to experience. This route travels through a scenic portion of the Bradford Ranger District—the forest's northern section—and offers access to major attractions like the Allegheny Reservoir and the Kiasutha Recreation Area. It's

What's left of the old Kinzua Bridge

an ideal way to experience the forest if you have at least a half day to spare, which is enough time for a few hikes and a little swimming.

It's a mostly uneventful drive between Smethport and the Allegheny National Forest; you'll pass a couple motorcycle clubs, lumber yards, and a correctional facility. When you reach small village of **Orsby,** look for signs touting a 4-mile detour south along State Road 3011 to **Kinzua Bridge State Park.** This is a side trip worth taking. Like all the state's best parks, Kinzua is equal parts beauty and intrigue. The centerpiece is the Kinzua Bridge, or at least what's left of it. Constructed in 1882, the bridge was crucial to the region's economic engine but was built prior to the wide-spread use of steel. The Kinzua was closed for good in 2002, and not a moment too soon: just a year later an F-1 tornado tore through the valley and blasted the bridge's middle section to pieces. Since that time, the state has gradually cleaned up the site, though much of the rubble and fallen timber remains. Two overlooks offer perfect views of what's left of the bridge, which is poignant evidence of what 100 mph winds can do. The intact bridge was beautiful (see the pictures on display near the overlook), but the rubble is mysteriously attractive as well. The commonwealth has begun renovating Kinzua Bridge State Park by stabilizing the viaduct's remaining pillars. The renovated park will allow visitors access to the still-standing portion of the bridge, for an even more exceptional view than what's offered now.

Continuing back on PA 59 west, pass **Marshburg,** the only town of any size along this segment and a gateway to the national forest. Just down the road is the Timberdoodle Flats Interpretive Trail, an easy family-oriented hike that offers guidance on spotting wildlife and is a pleasant way to kick off a day in the forest. Past Timberdoodle is the Bradford Ranger Station—home base for the forest's northern half and the place to pick up maps and ask for hiking, fishing, or boating suggestions. Since the district is more than a quarter million acres large, there is plenty to do. Many hikes in the Bradford District can be completed in a couple hours, and rangers are happy to make recommendations.

The route continues east and soon begins a breathtaking descent across the James Morrison Memorial Bridge, which runs over the **Allegheny Reservoir.** The reservoir is a 12,000-acre lake created by the Army Corps of Engineers that dammed this part of the Allegheny River in 1965 to manage flooding. At the bridge's base is **Docksiders Café,** which has some great deck tables overlooking the reservoir and marina. On the other side of the road is Kinzua Beach, a small strip of sand beach with a nice view of the reservoir and the Morrison Memorial Bridge. And just down the road is the imposing **Kinzua Dam** itself, which stands 177 feet from top to bottom. Here you'll find an information center and small hiking trail originating near the reservoir off PA 59.

If you continue farther down 59 and switch to the US 6 Business Route west (about 7 miles in total), you'll hit **Warren:** a small, attractive riverside city that profited from the fruits of the region's oil and lumber booms while maintaining its unique importance as a county seat. In addition to diners and sporting goods stores, Warren has as fun little coffeehouse and music venue (**The Crossing**) and some unusual shops like the Allegheny Book Mart, where comics, used books, and other curiosities complement Army surplus stock. Fine architecture in Warren has been attentively preserved; the striking brownstone flatiron bank building at the business district's major intersection is one obvious example, but the residences justify a look as well. Worth taking on its own merits, the 7-mile detour to Warren makes even more sense if you need to pick up provisions for a day (or more) in the forest, since it's easily the largest town in the vicinity.

If you do not wish to take the detour along PA 59 past the dam and into Warren, be on the lookout for the LONGHOUSE NATIONAL SCENIC BYWAY sign, which will appear *immediately* (perhaps 10 feet) after crossing the Morrison Memorial Bridge. Make the left turn and embark on a roller-coaster-style ride up and down the byway's high elevation. Stick to the 35 mph speed limit, which is there for your protection.

It's an eventful 6 miles on the byway, which hugs the southern leg of the reservoir. The water here is neatly tucked into scenic forest surroundings, but it's a large enough body to allow for an enjoyable sailing or powerboat excursion. Bring your rod and reel; record-breaking-sized pike and wall-eye have been caught in the reservoir. There are two boat launches along the byway—the Elijah Launch, which also allows fishing off the shore, and then Kiasutha, where a $5 parking fee buys you access to the lake, a sand beach, and a picnic area. **Kiasutha Recreation Area** is also the largest camping area in the forest, with close to a hundred sites. You'll pay a little extra for setting up on a lakefront site, but it's worth it.

Exit the forest and make a right onto PA 321. Pass Bob's Trading Post (not bad for pizza and a casual sit-down meal). The route meets US 6 briefly and continues south past **Kane**—a mountaintop frontier town founded by Thomas L. Kane, a friend of Civil War general and President

Ulysses S. Grant, and the man who recruited the celebrated Bucktail Regiment of the Pennsylvania Reserve Corps (see chapter 7 for more on the Bucktails). The town has dubbed itself the Black Cherry Capital of the World, which is a reference to the trees that surround Kane. Its business district is on US 6, making it a short detour off the route.

Kane is an interesting place. At more than 2,000 feet above sea level, the town feels a little more isolated than it really is. An unfortunate number of storefronts are boarded up, though signs of new investment can be found. Most notable are the unique food purveyors and eateries. Along Fraley Street (US 6), Bell's Meat & Poultry sells excellent homemade sausage, produce, and a variety of specialty cheeses, while Szymanski Bar and Restaurant is a good choice for dinner. And just footsteps off US 6 on Field Street, Texas Hot Lunch makes a terrific hot dog slathered in sauce. On the lodging front, ongoing rehabilitation of the stately **Kane Manor Country Inn** makes it an increasingly attractive place to spend the night.

After exploring Kane, continue along PA 321. You'll pass a historical marker for the Seneca Indian Spring, which references the now completely dislocated Seneca tribe that once inhabited the region extending from northwest Pennsylvania to western New York. A member tribe of the Six Nation Iroquois, the diplomatically skillful and militarily formidable Seneca played a key role in the development of the region (especially in oil country—see chapter 8) and outlasted the Lenape as a tribal presence in the state. The last Pennsylvania Seneca were forced out during construction of the Kinzua Dam in 1961.

A little bit past the spring marker, roughly 6 miles south of Kane, is one last chance to hike the national forest. There's a trailhead for the Twin Lakes Trail off PA 321, after a short detour down a forest road. This one is designed for backpackers, and a straight 16 miles west through the hardwood-rich wilderness to the Tionesta Scenic Area in the heart of the forest.

Cross the Clarion River, a meandering tributary of the Allegheny, and enter **Wilcox,** the gateway to Elk County and another old lumber town where the tanning industry thrived as well. Make the switch here to US 219 south. A deceptively long side trip along two roads (follow the signs) takes you to the Winery at Wilcox. The winery imports its grapes from North East, Pennsylvania (see chapter 8), which means an emphasis on sweet wines. Their Clarion River Red variety, served chilled, is a summer treat and popular locally.

Six miles past Wilcox, US 219 dips into **Johnsonburg.** Once powered by a diverse industrial base that included tanning and brick making, Johnsonburg now depends heavily on the paper industry. This is apparent immediately; access to the town on 219 runs straight past the sprawling Domtar paper mill. From the mill to Johnsonburg's peak elevations, the side streets follow a very steep grade. Neighborhoods and commercial blocks fill out the mountainside.

This three-thousand-person borough was actually the first settlement in Elk County, though its inaccessibility from the east kept things quiet for several decades prior to the Civil War, when western migration picked up and the town took off. Its geography was especially well suited to the lumber era. Johnsonburg's location amid the north-central forests on the Clarion River and near the Pittsburgh & New York Railroad made it a logical place to cluster the production processes associated with paper making. By 1900 Johnsonburg boasted the country's largest paper mill. Interestingly, the paper industry has shown relatively strong endurance in Pennsylvania (not just in Johnsonburg). The economics make sense: trees are again plentiful in North America, and while great cost savings may be achieved by importing expensive durable goods from foreign markets, the savings do not hold for inexpensive nondurable goods like paper.

> Johnsonburg holds claim to a strong patriotic tradition. No place in America sent a greater percentage of its population to fight in World War II—20 percent of Johnsonburg served overseas, according to the Elk County Historical Society. And the town and its hardworking populous carry on, having survived multiple floods and a postindustrial population decline.

Ten miles south from Johnsonburg along the Clarion River is **Ridgway,** Elk County's handsome county seat, settled by a Quaker merchant whose ancestors arrived in colonial America before Pennsylvania's founding. With his roots in the state's southeast region, Jacob Ridgway's town followed the systematic layout pioneered by William Penn in Philadelphia. Economic development followed a longer, more gradual trajectory in Ridgway than in other north-central towns. Johnsonburg's founding predates that of Ridgway, but sawmills came to Ridgway first, and the wages of stable, robust industrial investment followed. Ridgway became a haven for immigrants by the latter half of the 19th century, including an unusually large Swedish population. A thoroughly diverse industrial base included everything from standard lumber operations to cigar factories and silk

Main Street, Ridgway

mills. White-collar pursuits thrived as well, and Ridgway emerged as an influential regional banking center.

Great architecture fills the historic district. The variety of manufacturing operations meant an unusually large percentage of building materials could be procured from local firms; many Ridgway buildings are made of hardwoods, bricks, and stone from the immediate area. Described as "fresh and pleasing" by the WPA guidebook in 1940, the description holds to this day. As the county seat and an entryway to Elk County, Ridgway also supports an active **historical society** and the **Ridgway–Elk County Chamber of Commerce.** The welcome center at the latter's office (just across the street from the courthouse) is a good orientation point and information source.

Ridgway is an old village by Elk County standards but feels very much alive. If you look for them, you'll find reminders of the town's more prosperous past, such as the now vacant Opera House, which stayed open as the Strand movie theater through the early 1980s. But apart from the occasional hotel or theater, most buildings remain in use. Look for the **Towers Victorian Inn**, a fine bed & breakfast once occupied by a 19th-century lumber baron. Ridgway also has a couple good restaurants and food purveyors. **Lumberjack Steak & Seafood** serves high-quality, affordable meals; up the street a couple blocks, Two Scoops ice cream fountain is a tasty throwback.

IN THE AREA

Accommodations

There are more than 650 camping sites throughout Allegheny National Forest, as well as several private campgrounds in the vicinity. A small handful of bed & breakfasts can be found in towns like Kane and Ridgway.

Kane Manor Country Inn, 230 Clay Street, Kane. Call 814-837-6522. A cavernous country manse a few side roads away from Fraley Street. Low rack rates make this a bona fide bargain. Web site: www.kanemanor.com.

Towers Victorian Inn, 330 South Street, Ridgway. Call 814-772-7657. An impressive Italianate mansion in the heart of Ridgway with six rooms and a carriage house suite. Constructed at the height of the 19th-century lumber boom and beautifully furnished. Web site: www.towersinn.com.

Attractions and Recreation

Allegheny National Forest, 4 Farm Colony Drive, Warren. Call 814-723-5150. Web site: www.fs.fed.us/r9/forests/allegheny.

Elk County Historical Society, 109 Center Street, Ridgway. Call 814-776-1032. Open Wed.–Fri., Apr.–Nov., as well as Sat., June–Aug. The historical society has a small museum inside. Web site: www.elkcounty historicalsociety.org.

Kiasutha Recreation Area, part of Allegheny National Forest. Web site: www.fs.fed.us/r9/forests/allegheny/recreation/camping/kiasutha/.

Kinzua Bridge State Park, Johnsonburg. Call 814-965-2646. Web site: www.dcnr.state.pa.us/stateparks/parks/kinzuabridge.aspx.

Dining and Nightlife

The Crossing, 350 Pennsylvania Avenue W., Warren. Call 814-723-1771. A coffeehouse/music venue with a limited (but high-quality) lunch and dessert menu. Web site: www.thecrossingwarren.com.

Docksiders Café, PA 59, Warren. Call 814-726-9645. Great views from the deck; food is standard fare, but it's a great spot for cold drinks on a summer day. Open for lunch and dinner. Web site: www.kinzuamarina .com/cafe.htm.

Lumberjack Steak & Seafood, 102 Main Street, Ridgway. Call 814-772-9544. Offers burgers, salads, sandwiches, and an extensive dinner menu in a decor properly classified as "upscale rustic." A colorful mural detailing the region's lumber history wraps around the bar and lounge area. Open for lunch and dinner.

Other Contacts

Allegheny National Forest Visitors Bureau, 3183 Route 219, Foote Rest Campground Complex, Lantz Corners. Call 800-473-9370. Web site: www.visitanf.com.

Ridgway–Elk County Chamber of Commerce, 300 Main Street, Ridgway. Call 814-776-1424. Web site: www.ridgwaychamber.com.

A Bucktail tribute in Driftwood

CHAPTER

7

Great Forests— Part 2

Estimated length: 112 miles
Estimated time: 1 day

Getting there: Begin in Ridgway and drive down PA 120 east to St. Marys. From St. Marys, pick up PA 255 south down to Weedville. Turn onto PA 555 east and follow until the route terminates at the PA 120 intersection. Take 120 east again through the north-central Pennsylvania forests all the way to Lock Haven.

Highlights: This ride provides a rare chance to spot wild elk grazing and views of the vast open spaces that characterize the scenic north-central region. There are population clusters around handsome St. Marys (founded by German refugees), the old railroading village of Renovo, and Lock Haven on the Susquehanna banks.

Since its founding, Pennsylvania has been a haven for immigrants. William Penn experienced bigotry firsthand as a Quaker in Anglican England and established a tolerant ethos toward immigrants in Pennsylvania that outlasted the injustices committed by his descendants against the Native Americans. Driving around rural Pennsylvania centuries later, it is often possible to appreciate how immigrant groups shaped their settlements after the industrial age economic boom drew families from all corners of

Decker's Chapel, among the smallest in the United States

Europe. Even as American life trends the other way—towards conformity in people, homogeneity in culture, and even as small towns increasingly offer the same stores and restaurants—genuine local identity survives in places all over Pennsylvania. Sometimes the more enduring features of American life—architecture, government, religion, and schools, for example—manage to preserve this identity or at least create historical consciousness.

This is how two Elk County towns founded within 20 years and 10 miles of one another can feel so different, even today. Ridgway (where the last drive ended and this drive begins) and **St. Marys** (east of Ridgway on

PA 120) share a parallel economic history, grounded in lumbering and broadened by auxiliary industries like tanning and building materials production. But a radically different cultural heritage made these towns into very different places. Ridgway was founded mainly for commercial purposes by a Quaker businessman from the east and built as a small town Philadelphia on the state's western frontier. St. Marys was an asylum—a colony settled by German Catholics from Baltimore and Philadelphia in 1842 to escape the creeping religious bigotry that had taken hold in urban precincts where immigration trends unnerved the Protestant majority. This was an ugly moment in American history, as the nativist politics popularized by the Know Nothing movement were becoming an increasingly mainstreamed view. Meanwhile, political unrest in Germany fueled continued immigration to America. From its creation, the small St. Marys settlement by Elk Creek, blessed with arable farmland, ready access to clean water, and flush with virgin timber, had little trouble attracting inhabitants. Irish Catholics followed the Germans some 20 years later, changing the town's cultural identity slightly while reinforcing its religious character.

And much of this is evident in St. Marys today. Religious landmarks are one element, including downtown's St. Joseph's Monastery (the country's oldest Benedictine women's convent) and Decker's Chapel (often cited as the country's smallest church). From an economic standpoint, the town's endurance is at least partially owed to the community's inclination toward reinvestment within its borders. Its business leaders foresightedly diversified the town's industrial base amid the lumber boom, and manufacturing persists as an economic engine. Today, St. Marys is among the most prosperous places in the north-central region, and community pride is readily apparent. It is also an attractive place. A well-landscaped diamond-shaped public square forms the town's center, which is surrounded by shops and the twin-screen Apollo Theatre on the north side. Interestingly, the railroad also runs through the heart of town, where the business district is made up largely of independent stores. Just south of the tracks is the venerable **Gunners Inn and Restaurant.**

A favorite attraction in St. Marys is the **Straub Brewery,** which is among the oldest breweries in Pennsylvania. The family-run company makes distinctive, preservative-free microbrews in the same facility that founder Peter Straub opened in 1872. It can be hard to find Straub beer outside of Pennsylvania—the company only ships to distributors within a limited radius, though they've been expanding their geographical reach a little more as of late. Take the brewery tour on weekday mornings and learn the beer-making process in reverse; production begins on the higher floors, and the tour goes bottom to top. Time your visit right, and you may be offered a bottle of the freshest brew you'll ever drink, straight off the line. Either way, you're still invited to taste free beer from Straub's "Eternal Tap" on the second level. The brewery's dark beer is a flavorful treat, beloved even by those who dislike dark beers generally. Just remember to clean your glass when you're done.

Leaving St. Marys, travel south on PA 255 across a few suburban miles and emerge in a more satisfyingly rural piece of Elk County. After a brief incline, descend gradually toward **Byrnedale.** A mile and a half past this very small village, look for signs indicating PA 555. You'll have to make a very sharp left (almost a 180-degree turn) to get on 555. This route is one segment of a commonwealth-designated scenic drive that parallels the Bennett Branch of Sinnemahoning Creek. The stream, teeming with potential, is also teeming with acid mine drainage; treatment has helped somewhat, but it remains one of few waterways in this region avoided by fishermen. But fear not: later on in the drive are chances to visit magnificent wilderness waterways like First Fork Sinnemahoning Creek and Kettle Creek.

The approach to **Weedville** marks the beginning of the elk-spotting portion of the drive. Weedville and her surrounding villages are the heart of Pennsylvania's elk territory, for which the county is named. In early America, these large native deer grazed the mountainous Pennsylvania Wilds freely. A once-abundant population declined precipitously as settlement spread west; overhunting and environmental disruption followed the lumber boom, and the last elk was killed around 1867. In 1913, the state reintroduced the elk into Pennsylvania, importing animals from Yellowstone National Park in Montana and Wyoming. After a shaky beginning, the species has become a significant, stable presence in Elk and Cameron counties, with around eight hundred animals spread throughout. The October 2010 opening of the 8,400-square-foot **Elk Country Visitor Center** acknowledged the increasing visibility and public interest in Pennsylvania elk spotting. Lodging options like the cabins at **Wapiti Woods** cater to visitors from all corners of the state.

There is a strategy to finding elk in the Pennsylvania Wilds. The key is obtaining good intelligence, which can come from anyone—store owners, restaurateurs, hoteliers, other visitors, or area residents. When you arrive in **Benezette,** stop in at the **Benezette Hotel** or the Benezett Store & Restaurant (also the town's only gas station and the last opportunity you'll have to fill the tank for another 50 miles). Buy a snack or soda and ask offhandedly where the elk have been roaming that day. Keep in mind that during the warmer months the animals tend to come out at dawn and dusk when temperatures are low, making summer a notoriously difficult season for elk spotting. The herd's movements also depend on the mating cycle. Early fall is a prime time for seeing elk, as the breeding season is in full swing (September to October) and bulls make loud noises (called "bugling"), which give up their location. Elk tend to graze more openly during the early autumn as well.

That said, spotting Pennsylvania wildlife is never a sure thing. Hikers can spend years trekking through state parks looking for black bears and bald eagles in vain. But an elk sighting is an attainable goal, especially if you are willing to put in a little time. Aside from chance roadside encounters or tips from the locals, the best places to look are designated spots like the **Winslow Hill Elk Viewing Area,** which is a few miles off PA 555, north of Benezette. A low wooden fence separates elk spotters from the rolling fields where the herds roam. Ten miles east of Benezette on PA 555 is the Hicks Run viewing area, which includes an observational blind. Notable birdlife can be found here as well. No matter where you stop to look for elk, it helps to have binoculars.

In the interests of full disclosure, I'll confess that in four separate attempts I have yet to see an elk. The realities of scheduling have not always allowed me to follow the cardinal rules religiously, and I may lack the patience required for elk spotting. Regardless, this drive is among my favorites, and the PA 555 segment is its most picturesque stretch. The highway has been built inconspicuously into the natural scenery, and the scale of the Allegheny Plateau casts awe-inspiring insignificance onto passing cars. Hawks and ospreys circle overhead, fireflies invade the pitch-black nighttime skies, and the anticipation of an elk spotting lends extra excitement. The towns are few and far between, so speed limits go up to 55 mph, giving the car a chance to stretch its legs a little bit. Be safe and do keep a lookout for animals near the roadside. But elk or no elk, the mountain vistas around the Pennsylvania Wilds are beautiful.

Shortly after the Hicks Run viewing area is a nerve-racking diversion.

Look for signs indicating the **Fred Woods Trail,** which involves a left turn, 4 miles off PA 555. The trail is a somewhat difficult 4.5-mile hike through **Elk State Forest,** distinguished by the large and beautiful boulders scattered throughout this heavily wooded elevated area. But the real adventure is the harrowing drive up to the trailhead along steep, rocky, and unpredictable Mason Hill Road, which lacks guardrails. For the faint of heart, it helps to have a four-wheel-drive vehicle.

PA 555 terminates in **Driftwood,** which is almost completely encircled by mountains. It's an interesting effect; look around for a moment, and you'll feel as though you're at the bottom of the world's largest soup bowl. Driftwood is a very small town, but home to some great Civil War history. It was here where the famed Bucktail Regiment of the Pennsylvania Reserve Corps began its journey eastward—a prelude to its brave service in support of the Union cause. Led by Lieut. Col. Thomas L. Kane (founder of Kane— see chapter 6), the Bucktails were northwest and north-central Pennsylvania lumbermen and farmers whose hunting experience proved extraordinarily useful on the battlefield. A monument to the Bucktails stands at the center of Driftwood near a small playground.

Where PA 555 ends, it intersects with PA 120, nicknamed the Bucktail Highway to honor the regiment's contribution to the war effort. Follow the highway east. The remainder of the drive runs along this highway through the heart of the north-central forests and offers several opportunities for adventuresome detours. Just past Driftwood is an access point for the Bucktail Path, a 32-mile hike through Elk State Forest that's popular with elk-spotting backpackers. Soon after, the highway intersects PA 872, which you may wish to take north to **Sinnemahoning State Park** alongside beautiful First Fork Sinnemahoning Creek, famous for its large trout. And then farther down the road is a side trip to **Kettle Creek State Park,** 9 miles off the highway from the minuscule town of **Westport.** Like First Fork Sinnemahoning, Kettle Creek is a trout fisherman's paradise, particularly in and around the lake area created by a large dam.

The only town of any size along this segment is **Renovo** ("to renew" in Latin), which is 24 miles east of Driftwood in Clinton County. Renovo's roots are with the Philadelphia & Erie Railroad (the P&E), which opened repair shops here in 1863. The town was built for the shops' employees, and other manufacturing industries sprung up shortly thereafter. The P&E was soon swallowed by the Pennsylvania Railroad (PRR) and the repair facilities continued operating through the eleventh hour of the PRR's decline, closing in 1982. Renovo has had difficulty coping with this disinvestment, unfortunately evident in the tired business district, which faces the repair shops and runs along Erie Avenue. The good news is that the shops were reopened by a new private railcar repair company.

One thing Renovo has going for it is a unique location, wedged neatly into **Sproul State Forest**—at 280,000 acres, the largest state-owned forest in Pennsylvania, named for the governor who hired Gifford Pinchot as the state forest commissioner. Known for its cold-water trout fishing (Kettle Creek closely neighbors the forest), Sproul is bisected by the West Branch of the Susquehanna River. Oak trees grace the mountainsides and become a fiery tapestry of reds, oranges, and yellows in the autumn. To mark the occasion, Renovo hosts the **Pennsylvania State Flaming Foliage Festival** every October. The program includes a parade, beauty contest, and chance to appreciate the fall leaves changing colors from an idyllic location amid the mountains. Nine miles northeast from Renovo, **Hyner Run State Park** is a great spot to go for scenic autumn views and a fine fishing destination as well.

From here, the Bucktail Highway goes another 20 miles and terminates in **Lock Haven,** a nine-thousand-person town perched on the banks of the West Branch Susquehanna River. As a destination and transfer point for large quantities of felled lumber acquired throughout the region's forests, Lock Haven is a fitting end to the network of drives along the state's north-central region. Its location sealed its destiny as a transportation hub—raw materials and goods flowed naturally from riverside towns along the West Branch through Lock Haven and down the Susquehanna into Maryland. The name references the locks associated with the West Branch Canal, a feeder route into the Main Line of Public Works, which eventually connected Philadelphia to Pittsburgh.

If the Susquehanna helped build Lock Haven, it also posed an existential threat. A devastating flood in 1972 eventually led to the construction of a levee and other new development along the banks, like a paved river walk and sand beach. Five-thousand-student Lock Haven University is a major presence around town, but there are also a fair share of dimly lit bars where the old-timers hang out. As the Clinton County seat, Lock Haven sports a Romanesque courthouse in the downtown historic district, based around Water Street. Notable buildings are mainly Victorian in style.

IN THE AREA

Accommodations

Benezette Hotel, 95 Winslow Hill Road, Benezette. Call 814-787-4240. Simple, reliable accommodations at the nexus of elk spotting in Pennsylvania. Web site: www.benezettehotel.com.

Wapiti Woods, PA 555, Weedville. Call 814-787-7525. Nicely appointed cabins ensconced in elk country, rentable by the night or week (two-night minimum on weekends). Web site: www.wapitiwoods.com.

Attractions and Recreation

Elk Country Visitor Center, 134 Homestead Drive, Benezette. Call 814-787-5167. Web site: www.elkcountryvisitorcenter.com.

Elk State Forest, 258 Sizerville Road, Emporium. Call 814-486-3353. Web site: www.dcnr.state.pa.us/forestry/stateforests/elk.aspx.

Hyner Run State Park, 86 Hyner Park Road, North Bend. Call 570-923-6000. Web site: www.dcnr.state.pa.us/stateparks/parks/hynerrun.aspx.

Kettle Creek State Park, 97 Kettle Creek Park Lane, Renovo. Call 570-923-6004. Web site: www.dcnr.state.pa.us/stateparks/parks/kettlecreek .aspx.

Pennsylvania State Flaming Foliage Festival, 2132 Woodland Avenue, Renovo. Call 570-923-2411.

Sinnemahoning State Park, 8288 First Fork Road, Austin. Call 814-647-8401. Web site: www.dcnr.state.pa.us/stateparks/parks /sinnemahoning.aspx.

Sproul State Forest, 15187 Renovo Road, Renovo. Call 570-923-6011. Web site: www.dcnr.state.pa.us/forestry/stateforests/sproul.aspx.

Straub Brewery, 303 Sorg Street, St. Marys. Call 814-834-7628. Tours are Mon.–Fri., mornings. Web site: www.straubbeer.com.

Dining and Nightlife

Gunners Inn and Restaurant, 33 South Street, St. Marys. Call 814-834-2161. Live piano music, steaks, chops, and quality pub food at this friendly downtown restaurant with an attached 24-room motel. And it's in St. Marys, so fresh-brewed Straub is a must. Open for lunch and dinner. Web site: www.gunners.biz.

Other Contacts

Pennsylvania Wilds Tourism Marketing Corporation. Call 800-577-2029. Web site: www.pawilds.com.

Lighthouse at Presque Isle

CHAPTER

8

The Erie Hook

Estimated length: 80 miles
Estimated time: 1 day

Getting there: The drive begins in North East, Pennsylvania (somewhat confusingly, as this is the northwest portion of the state—the name refers to the town's placement within the county). Head west along PA 5, and take Alternate PA 5 to go through Erie. PA 5 ends in Erie County's Springfield Township. Take US 20 east briefly, then continue on US 6N east all the way through to the college town of Edinboro.

Highlights: This fun little jaunt around the far northwest offers wine tasting along the Chautauqua–Lake Erie Wine Trail, cool breezes on the sandy shores of Presque Isle State Park, and the underappreciated cultural assets of Erie city.

Among the more wonderful trends to take hold throughout Pennsylvania in recent years is the state's long-overdue willingness to silence its inner teetotaler. This minor betrayal of Pennsylvania's abstemious Quaker heritage has been a peaceful revolution, but a revolution nonetheless. Seemingly overnight, brand new microbreweries serving unique, delicious beers have cropped up in every corner of the state. Of course, beer making is hardly new to Pennsylvania—Founding Fathers were drinking Philadelphia ale at

Among the many rolling vineyards of North East

the Constitutional Convention, and brands like Yuengling and Straub can trace their origins to the 19th century. More dramatic has been the explosion in wine production. There are now more than 130 wineries here, nearly half of which opened during the last decade. Pennsylvania turns out a million gallons of wine annually, making it the fifth biggest wine producing state in the country. If only we could eliminate the state liquor control board, we'd be all set.

This trip begins in the heart of Pennsylvania's wine country near the shores of Lake Erie in **North East.** This cheery little town is just a few miles from the New York state border and the southern point of the Chautauqua–Lake Erie Wine Trail. The trail is the world's second largest Concord and Niagara grape belt next to Napa Valley, with more than 30,000

acres of farmland in western New York and northwest Pennsylvania devoted to grape growing. And it's not just about the wine. A Welch's grape juice
processing plant opened in North East in 1911, predating most of the vineyards and helping to establish grapes as the region's keystone cash crop.
Sadly, while you can tour and taste all along the wine trail, the Welch's plant
is closed to the public.

Why all the grapes? Climate is the main reason—Lake Erie moderates
temperatures year-round, meaning consistently mild winter and summer
seasons, which are ideal for the vineyards. The rocky soil is also very kind to
grape cultivation. And despite an increasingly challenging marketplace for
Pennsylvania farmers, grape growing has proven itself an economically sustainable activity.

Harvest season in September and October is a fine time to visit, as several vineyards offer tours and the town holds a wine festival. There are
currently eight wineries in North East, with another dozen or so across
the state line in New York. Though it lacks the fanfare of Napa, the Chautauqua–Lake Erie Wine Trail is a popular regional getaway in summer and
fall, attracting western New Yorkers, Pennsylvanians, and Ohioans in
droves. The town supports a fair share of lodging options, from no-frills
chain hotels to the select **Grape Arbor Bed and Breakfast.**

North East wines tend toward the sweet and fruity. If this is what you're
after, start with a visit to South Shore Wine Company, which offers a wide
variety of berry-infused specialty wines. South Shore is also North East's
most historic facility, offering tastings in a stone-walled cellar that dates
back more than 150 years, when they first began winemaking here. The
property has changed ownership several times since then and endured
everything from poor growing seasons to Prohibition. It is now in the capable hands of the Mazza family, which owns a second winery in North East
and a third in western New York.

Several wineries use local vineyards to make ice wine—a chilly, syrupy
creation made from grapes harvested in the winter. Ice wines are tougher to
produce and have a higher price point than your average chardonnay or
cabernet sauvignon, but most wineries in North East will let you sample
one for a buck. Personally speaking, the ice wines give me a headache after
a glass or two. Balance things out a bit and taste some nice oak-aged dry
reds at Lakeview Wine Cellars, which is located a little bit south off the
main wine trail. Lakeview opened in 2008 and features a wine-bottle-
shaped lake.

The wine trail dissipates as PA 5 leaves North East. The route remains scenic, however, with rolling grape farms occupying the landscape on the south side and the lake's shore close by on the north. One nice place to stop is Shades Beach Park, 8 miles from North East, which offers a boat launch, playground, and picnic area. The shore is occupied mostly by rocks, but sand beaches appear farther along the drive at Presque Isle.

Follow the PA 5 alternate route into **Erie,** which feels far too intimate to be Pennsylvania's fourth-largest city. Nevertheless, with a population hovering at just more than a hundred thousand people, that's exactly what it is. Named for the Eriez Indians who lived in the region prior to European colonization and war with the Iroquois, this comfortable lakefront municipality is one of a few intermediate-sized Pennsylvania cities that has managed to preserve the architecture and character that marked its industrial age growth spurt. A peaceful town with wide avenues and large blocks, Erie served dual purposes to the state and the region: first as a manufacturing hub along the Great Lakes shipping network, and second as an accessible getaway destination, known for its short but pleasant summers. The central thoroughfare between Buffalo and Detroit, Lake Erie became especially crucial to the American economy after the New York canal system came into its own and extended shipping access to its major cities. During this time the city of Erie was a vital contributor to the supply chain, exporting, refining, and producing durable goods from western Pennsylvania's abundant natural resources.

The city's industrial presence has downscaled gradually, but the cool summer breezes and natural sandy beaches remain. So does the city's neighborly disposition, exemplified in its long-standing civic institutions. It's a bit of a cliché, but no Pennsylvania city of comparable size feels more like a small town.

PA 5 becomes E. Sixth Street as you cross the city limits and encounter Perry Square, which interrupts the roadway and is guarded by a statue of Cdre. Oliver Hazard Perry. An American hero whose likeness appears all over town, Perry achieved a significant victory over the British in the War of 1812 at the Battle of Lake Erie. Formerly a lieutenant, Perry had volunteered for the thankless task of building ships on the lake in an effort to establish a naval presence in the region and reacquire American territory. During the battle, he lost his flagship, *Lawrence,* and made a tactically clever switch to the *Niagara,* from which he defeated the British fleet. The aftereffects of the battle were especially difficult—trying to repair Perry's ships during the bone-chilling winters led to more deaths, which is why an adjacent inlet came to be known as Misery Bay.

The battle lives on at the **Erie Maritime Museum** with its signature attraction: a reconstructed U.S. Brig *Niagara.* The original version had a tumultuous postwar history. She was sunk in Misery Bay after the battle, recovered in 1913, sunk again due to neglect in 1929, recovered once more, and gradually restored. But the original ship could not be completely refurbished, so a replica was commissioned in 1988. The new version is a magnificent, fully functional ship. When it's not docked at the museum, the *Niagara* is often sailing around the region and appearing at tall boats festivals. You can even sign up to work aboard the ship; the *Niagara* accepts novice sailors to accompany

The rebuilt Brig Niagara *leaving Erie for a festival in Cleveland*

the professionals on voyages as part of the Live Aboard Trainee program.

The maritime museum is located in the Bayfront area, a major redevelopment site that is home to a convention center (built in 2007) and the **Sheraton Erie Bayfront Hotel** (built in 2008). In 1996, the Erie-Western Port Authority completed the 184-foot-high **Bicentennial Tower,** located just down the street, to commemorate Erie's two-hundred-year anniversary. The low admission fee is well worth paying for the bird's-eye views of Presque Isle and the city. On clear days you can see 20 miles across the lake into Canada.

Downtown Erie is relatively compact, so park the car somewhere and walk around a little. State Street is the main downtown artery, and its northern blocks are close to most major attractions. It's where you'll find the **Erie Art Museum,** an imaginatively adapted Greek Revival bank building that is easily identified by its tall Doric columns and white marble façade. One great permanent feature is *The Avalon Restaurant,* a soft sculpture installation depicting the colorful characters who frequented the city's now-defunct diner. A few blocks away, the art deco **Warner Theatre** puts on concerts, dance recitals, and musicals against an elegant backdrop that achieves an ambience unique to the pre-Depression-era movie houses. Good restaurants are sprinkled throughout town; the **Brewerie** brewpub and **Pufferbelly Restaurant and Bar** are just a couple options, both housed in creatively adapted older buildings.

Explore Erie at your own pace. PA 5 offers easy access to both the Bayfront and State Street. On the west side of downtown, PA 5 passes the county courthouse and the stylish Victorian mansions of W. Sixth Street. A few have been converted to bed & breakfasts; the 24-room Romanesque-style **Watson-Curtze Mansion** became a museum for local artifacts and a planetarium. This "millionaires' row" extends west; drive through and approach the city limits, where a more suburban aesthetic takes hold and low-rise motels and small resorts begin to appear. Look for the Arby's—a good orientation point thanks to the oversized cowboy hat logo sign—which marks the intersection with Peninsula Drive (PA 832).

Make the right onto Peninsula—this is the entrance point to **Presque Isle State Park,** the pearl of northwest Pennsylvania and a bona fide national treasure. A feather-shaped peninsula, its name is owed to the French who inhabited the area through the mid-18th century and where they established a fort. The French named it Presq'uile, meaning "peninsula" or "almost an island"—accurate enough, as the park is attached to the city by a thin strip of land. A birdwatcher's paradise, Presque Isle's recreational opportunities extend to biking, swimming, fishing, canoeing, or simply sunning along the sandy beaches. On all but the most frigid winter days you'll find locals in-line skating, jogging, and walking their dogs along the 14-mile paved trail that loops around the park's perimeter. The state's most visited park, it is large enough and remote enough to sustain a peaceful ambience all year-round.

There's a lot to do. Hiking trails are laced throughout the park, designed to incorporate the many small ponds and wildlife-spotting areas that occupy the heart of the peninsula. Picnicking sites and historical curiosities abound. Note the 57-foot-high Presque Isle Lighthouse on the northern shorefront—visible from 13 nautical miles out, the facility was powered by oil lamp and required round-the-clock attention by its resident operator (the lighthouse now utilizes a 250-watt bulb). It is not to be confused with the old Waterworks gear tower on the south side of the park's neck, which brought potable Lake Erie water into the city during the early 20th century. Just across from the gear tower is a bike-rental concession where you can borrow standard bicycles as well as four-person surreys. Biking is a great way to see Presque Isle, thanks to the paved path around the shorelines and the narrow Sidewalk Trail that cuts through the middle section. Birding enthusiasts should ask a park ranger for recommended hikes. An astonishing variety of birdlife occupies Presque Isle (more than three hundred species have been spotted), and the park is a natural pass-through for migrating avian life. Presque Isle is basically flat, and hikes are easy and navigable.

In the summertime it's hard to beat the sandy beaches on the north side, where Lake Erie laps gently against the shore. The water disappears into the distance, as endless and unknown as the Atlantic Ocean appears from an East Coast beach. You can fish for trout from the beach, though many prefer angling off the piers that abut Presque Isle Bay. Commodore Perry makes his presence known on the southeast side of the peninsula where a monument to his heroism at the Battle of Lake Erie stands beside Misery Bay. Scenic boat tours take off from here as well.

The gateway to the park includes a couple notables. On the right is the **Tom Ridge Environmental Center,** named for the former director of Homeland Security, Pennsylvania governor, and onetime Erie-based congressman. The center is a modern, stylishly designed (and ecofriendly) facility that offers a thorough education on Presque Isle's complex ecosystems. You can also take a trip up the center's glass tower for superlative lake views over the roller coaster tracks at neighboring **Waldameer Park & Water World.** Waldameer is a family-friendly seasonal amusement and water park featuring more than 75 rides that range from carnival attractions for small children to classic wooden coasters. Admission is free, and an unlimited-ride pass is around $20 (half price after 6 PM). There's also a large midway with skee ball and a bank of nostalgia-inducing Twenty One machines, which were how I learned rudimentary blackjack when I was a kid.

With so much to do in and around Presque Isle, it makes sense to spend a full day. Food concessions are limited at the park, but there are several places to pick up lunch just off Peninsula Drive and along PA 5. Waldameer also serves burgers, hot dogs, and excellent French fries from its food kiosks. And the environmental center has a small café.

After Presque Isle, proceed west along PA 5 to **Avonia,** which is the next town over. If it's summer, look for satellite roadside locations of **Mason**

Waldameer coaster with Lake Erie in the background

Farms Country Market, where fresh corn, strawberries, raspberries, and other good produce are available. Enjoy the country scenery all the way through to **Lake City,** at which point Erie County turns largely rural. Catch one last view of the lake from Lake Erie Community Park or **Erie Bluffs State Park,** a 504-acre lakefront spot established in 2004 where you may see anglers who prefer the undeveloped shoreline to the crowds at Presque Isle. Trout fishermen also head down to Elk Creek, accessible from this part of PA 5 along a winding side route.

The PA 5/US 20 intersection occurs just a mile east of the Ohio state border at an abandoned service station. After a short distance on US 20 east, continue east on US 6N. This mostly rural stretch hits only two towns. The first is **Albion,** an old canal and railroad village. The second is much larger **Edinboro,** the route's terminating point, which appears after a developed stretch near the I-79 overpass (mostly chain restaurants and gas stations). Edinboro itself is a pleasant, seven-thousand-person college town home to Edinboro University of Pennsylvania, whose student population eclipses that of the borough. The name connects the university and the town to a wave of Scottish immigration that came to the area in the colonial era. The school is best known for its art degree programs, though its class offerings include most disciplines. Handsome brick buildings and well-tended grounds characterize the campus. A 245-acre lake on the north side of town made Edinboro an early resort destination and continues to offer scenic boating and fishing opportunities. A small downtown business district includes college hangouts (pizza parlors and pubs) as well as a handful of boutique shops.

IN THE AREA

Accommodations

Most varieties of lodging are available on this drive, with smaller inns and chain hotels found around North East and Erie alike. Peninsula Drive near the gateway to Presque Isle State Park is lined with motels and small resorts.

Grape Arbor Bed and Breakfast, 51 E. Main Street, North East. Call 866-725-0048. An early-Victorian-style inn with eight guest rooms and suites complemented by multiple common lounge areas to enjoy the local wine. Web site: www.grapearborbandb.com.

Sheraton Erie Bayfront Hotel, 55 W. Bay Drive, Erie. Call 814-454-2005. Two hundred contemporary rooms, furnished with flat-screen televisions and deluxe beds. Located on the water and adjacent to the city's convention center, the Sheraton draws both tourists and business travelers. A pool deck and patio are situated right on the bay. Web site: www.starwoodhotels.com.

Attractions and Recreation

Bicentennial Tower, 7 State Street, Erie. Call 814-455-6055.

Erie Art Museum, 411 State Street, Erie. Call 814-459-5477. Open Tues.–Sun., year-round. Web site: www.erieartmuseum.org.

Erie Bluffs State Park, 201 State Street, Erie. Call 814-833-7424. Web site: www.dcnr.state.pa.us/stateparks/parks/eriebluffs.aspx.

Erie Maritime Museum, 150 E. Front Street, Erie. Call 814-452-2744. Open daily, Apr.–Oct.; Thurs.–Sat., Nov.–Mar. Call ahead to confirm hours. Web site: www.flagshipniagara.org.

Mason Farms Country Market. Web site: www.masonfarms.net /sattelites.htm.

Presque Isle State Park, 301 Peninsula Drive, Erie. Call 814-833-7424. Web site: www.dcnr.state.pa.us/stateparks/parks/presqueisle.aspx.

Tom Ridge Environmental Center, 301 Peninsula Drive, Erie. Call 814-833-6050. Open daily, year-round. Web site: www.trecpi.org.

Waldameer Park & Water World, 220 Peninsula Drive, Erie. Call 814-838-3591. Open Tues.–Sun., June–Aug., as well as Fri.–Sun. in May and early Sept. Web site: www.waldameer.com.

Warner Theatre, 811 State Street, Erie. Call 814-452-4857.

Watson-Curtze Mansion, 356 W. Sixth Street, Erie. Call 814-871-5790. Web site: www.eriecountyhistory.org.

Dining and Nightlife

You can eat well in Erie, though cuisine doesn't venture too far from traditional American comfort food. Bayfront restaurants understandably emphasize seafood dishes.

The Brewerie, 123 W. Fourth Street, Erie. Call 814-454-2200. This restaurant and brewpub is located just off State Street but several blocks south of the bay on a somewhat isolated block. It's housed in the city's magnificent old Union Station, completely renovated and transformed into a restaurant. Several varieties are brewed on-site, complemented by bottled beers from regional brewers like the Erie Brewing Company (producer of the light and refreshing low-alcohol Presque Isle Pilsner). Open for lunch and dinner. Web site: www.brewerie.com.

Pufferbelly Restaurant and Bar, 414 French Street, Erie. Call 814-454-1557. Occupies a former firehouse and complements its salads, sandwiches, pastas, and chops with the second most comprehensive collection of fire department memorabilia in the city. (The most comprehensive is five blocks away at the Erie Firefighters Historical Museum.) Open for lunch, dinner, and Sun. brunch. Web site: www.thepufferbelly.com.

Other Contacts

Chautauqua–Lake Erie Wine Trail. Web site: www.chautauquawine trail.org.

VisitErie, 208 Bayfront Parkway, Erie. Call 800-524-3743. Web site: www.visiteriepa.com.

Decorative derricks in Oil City

CHAPTER

9

Old Energy, New Energy

Estimated length: 75 miles
Estimated time: 1–2 days

Getting there: Start in Oil City and travel north on PA 8 to Titusville. Proceed west on PA 27. Switch to PA 173 south in Mount Hope, and take it all the way to the end of the route. Turn right onto PA 8 for 0.1 mile, and then follow PA 528 south through Moraine State Park to the drive's conclusion in the small town of Prospect.

Highlights: This drive explores Pennsylvania's oil heritage, headquartered around Oil City and Titusville in the northwest. Though the boom is long past, the history is well preserved at the Drake Well Museum and Oil Creek State Park. The route soon gives way to the country scenery of Butler County, capped by beautiful Moraine State Park and Lake Arthur.

When one thinks of the American oil industry, states like Texas, Louisiana, and Alaska come to mind. But the first oil well in history was drilled into northwest Pennsylvania in the summer of 1859, just a few miles from a town called Titusville. Consider your motor oil's brand name the next time you put a quart of Quaker State or Pennzoil in your engine. Relatively little crude is pumped here anymore, but the American oil industry's roots are planted firmly in northwest Pennsylvania. For a short time in the latter half of the

19th century, the region was an oil-soaked bedlam of hastily constructed boomtowns with overflowing boardinghouses, gambling halls, bordellos, overnight millionaires, creeks saturated in crude, and wooden derricks running up and down the mountainside as far as the eye could see. Traveling around the Oil Region National Heritage Area (as the government has designated greater Venango County), you'll see some terrific photographs from the era portraying the mass chaos—oilmen and mules dripping in crude, makeshift tools on the muddy ground, derricks stacked behind one another like dominos, and so on. The fumes practically waft off the paper.

Pennsylvania crude is a little thinner and lighter than the Texas variety to which most are accustomed. And the original boom had nothing to do with powering automobiles, which had not been invented yet. In the 19th century, Americans were after anything that could power their lamps. Light was to the Civil War era as automotive travel is to modern times. And while the end product was kerosene rather than gasoline, the thirst for oil was just as intense.

Still, there was not always such tremendous demand. The Seneca Indians who inhabited the region and the white settlers who followed had discovered oil in pits and washed up on the banks of Oil Creek—a tributary of the Allegheny River. They gathered it unceremoniously and used the stuff as medicine. It was a good deal later that research on hydrocarbons suggested the true potential of crude. But the industry was highly speculative, and it had not occurred to anyone to drill for oil until a chemist named George Bissell developed the technique, modified from the drilling method used to extract salt. Nobody expected it to work. When Bissell sent Edwin Drake to Titusville in 1858, among his qualifications for the job was that as an erstwhile railroad employee Drake held a free train ticket.

But the incredulous townsfolk and East Coast industrialists stopped laughing when Drake hit oil at 69 feet below the surface and unleashed the oil boom. What came next was feverish growth, often compared to the pandemonium that came to California after the first golden nugget was found. Towns like Titusville and Cornplanter (named for the famed Seneca chief) were transformed from remote logging villages with a few dozen people each into 10,000-person cities within five years. Close by, cities like Pithole and Petroleum Center were born overnight. Homes were shabbily constructed on purpose—if oil was found beneath them, they would need to be torn down quickly. Civil War veterans, industrialists, rogues, and roughnecks all came to seek their fortune in oil. "Dippers" collected runoff

The Oil City countryside

on the creek banks and started their own oil businesses using the crude they could skim with pans and soak with blankets. Something like a thousand derricks were up at the boom's peak, though accurate estimates are notoriously difficult to come by since the numbers changed so frequently and nobody was really counting. Within a couple decades, John D. Rockefeller and Standard Oil had scooped most of it up anyway, forming the seminal American monopoly that led to the seminal antitrust lawsuit that forged the modern American oil industry.

Back in the 1860s, though, entrepreneurs built the Oil Creek Valley. Support industries cropped up along the riverbanks, attempting to feed and clothe the influx. Each town had a unique purpose. Bisected by Oil Creek where the tributary meets the Allegheny River, the area known as Cornplanter was renamed **Oil City** during the boom and emerged as a key transit hub for crude. This is where the route begins. "Teamsters" (no relation to the modern IBT union) gathered in Oil City to transport oil down-stream on the Allegheny to refineries in Pittsburgh. Railroads and pipelines quickly make the river obsolete as a means for moving crude, but Oil City remained a focal oil town for a long time. Until recently, it was the corporate headquarters for Pennzoil–Quaker State; the company was swallowed by Shell and moved to Texas in 2002.

Catch up on this history by visiting the **Venango Museum of Art, Science and Industry** in Oil City's converted beaux-arts post office. A meticulously balanced presentation (in a political sense) of the oil business is supplemented by some impressive local material. See a cream-colored 1937 Cord automobile and a Wurlitzer organ, which was moved here from the town's former theater and is as beautiful as it is functional. Ask a museum employee to have the organ play a song or two (it knows 20).

The departure of Pennzoil–Quaker State has been a challenge for Oil City, but the town has shown resilience. In recent years, it has aggressively marketed itself as a hot community for creative types. Two dozen artists keep studios downtown at the elegant Romanesque-style **National Transit Company Building** and its annex, while other newcomers have adapted Victorian homes into mixed-use studio and residential space. Artists are drawn by the low cost of living, tranquil riverside scenery, and targeted relocation sweeteners like home-buyers grants and tax abatements. The Transit building is open to the public, with gallery space and studios occupying two levels. A colorful two-wall mural in the foyer traces the arc of the region's oil-drilling history.

The building is a stop on the self-guided downtown walking tour, which also swings visitors along the creek-side Justus Park and Pennzoil's former headquarters at the art deco Drake Building. I've also enjoyed walking around the Northside residential historic district. It's a steep climb up to this Victorian-flavored neighborhood, but the homes are interesting, and the valley views are excellent. You'll also pass by the distinctive matching spires of St. Joseph's Convent, Rectory and Church, which are visible from almost anywhere in town.

A point that cannot be emphasized enough: despite the region's dalliance with oil drilling, including environmentally calamitous practices during the boom, greater Venango County is now quite pristine. A combination of cleanup efforts, tightened regulation, and environmental resilience has restored the Oil Creek Valley and her surrounding mountains to something approximating their primeval state.

You'll see this up close 3 miles north from Oil City at **Oil Creek State Park.** This long, thin swath of scenic parkland is split down the middle by the creek. The entrance from PA 8 leads drivers to the old Petroleum Center railroad station, which has been converted into a visitors center and exhibit space. The showpiece is a detailed diorama portraying the (now almost completely abandoned) town at the height of the oil boom. There are lots of interesting characters and stories to be told—even by the standards of the day, Petroleum Center was regarded as a lawless place.

The park is a fun and educational attraction. Scattered throughout are informational placards and tableau installations that reconstruct what the area used to look like. A wooden-planked walking path guides visitors through Petroleum Center in the wake of the oil boom. For the full experience, there's the 36-mile Gerard Hiking Trail, which encircles the entire

Visitors center in Oil Creek State Park, where abandoned Petroleum Center once stood

park. It's a little bit rugged, but it's a nice hike. The park also allows canoeing and fishing, hosts a summer biathlon, and features a 10-mile paved bike path connecting the south point to the north. Finally, if you're interested, 5 miles east of the park is the ghost town of **Pithole City,** which burned to the ground after the oil ran out.

The route meanders mostly around the state park, so investigate independently. When you're done, return to PA 8 and follow it north to **Titusville.** The site of Drake's first oil well is a little more than a mile from downtown at the north end of Oil Creek State Park. Titusville is one of few cities in the area that had significant white settlement prior to the arrival of industry, subsisting quietly as a small lumber town founded by surveyor Jonathan Titus in 1796. It became the most orderly, sophisticated part of the oil region, earning the moniker Queen City after the rough-and-tumble boom period had passed. As with Oil City, preserved Victorian homes and Colonial Revival structures are a reminder of the past. I particularly like the Algrunix Building and its unusual onion turret. While it

Erie National Wildlife Refuge

will likely never again see such an influx of wealth, Titusville is an agreeable place with a strong sense of community. Summer concerts at Scheide Park downtown and microbrews at the bright and airy **Blue Canoe Brewery** are just a couple favored pastimes.

Signs direct visitors to the major attractions, like the **Drake Well Museum** at the north end of Oil Creek State Park (also an entrance for the aforementioned bike path). At the end of 2010, the museum was in the midst of renovation but scheduled to reopen within a year. In the meantime there's a superb educational park behind the museum space that gets deep into the complexities of oil production. This area was a Civilian Conservation Corps project and features mock derricks, a pumping station, a modern steel rig, and the attention-getting Central Power Building, which pops noisily but was built to keep several wells pumping simultaneously. They've also rebuilt Drake's operation "board for board" atop his old well.

The other big attraction in Titusville is the **Oil Creek and Titusville Railroad** (or OC&T). Founded in 1986 by railroad enthusiasts, the OC&T purchased old, abandoned Pennsylvania Railroad tracks connecting the state's northwest oil region to the southwest steel region and to industrial centers in western New York. The historical society that operates the OC&T has re-created a terrific experience, supporting both freight rail and passenger rail. You can take advantage of the latter by purchasing a ticket aboard an old luxury Pullman coach and traveling the 26-mile round-trip, which runs through Oil Creek State Park and hits four stations along the way. Like other leisure railroads in Pennsylvania (New Hope, for example), the OC&T offers special themed rides, including a murder-mystery tour. Purchase tickets at the renovated train station in downtown Titusville that doubles as a large souvenir shop and orientation point for the whole Oil Region. Just across the street is the **Caboose Motel,** a string of railcars innovatively transformed into moderately priced accommodations.

Switch to PA 27 west from Titusville and follow this road 16 miles to the intersection at PA 173. Along the way you'll pass the bargain-priced Mount Hope Golf Course; the straightforward layout won't challenge experienced golfers, but the course is well maintained. Pick up PA 173 where it begins at the PA 27 intersection, and follow it south past the farms and fields of southern Crawford County. On the way, stop at the marshy **Erie National Wildlife Refuge,** renowned for its diverse and abundant birdlife. The Sugar Lake Division of the refuge is reachable from 173 if you pay close attention to the signs. Once you're in the refuge, look for the Observational

NATURAL GAS: THE NEXT BOOM?

Over the course of several years, the heart of the American oil industry migrated from Pennsylvania to Texas, as the drilling techniques developed in Titusville took the Texas oil fields by storm. More than a hundred years later, the Lone Star State seems intent on returning the favor with hydraulic fracturing and other advanced methods for tapping Pennsylvania's natural gas reserves. What this really means remains to be seen. These methods have brought with them the promise of revitalizing disinvested rural counties along with the potential to damage forests and farmland. It all depends on whom you ask.

Back in the early 1980s, a small oil and gas exploration company began experimenting with new gas exploration techniques in north Texas where substantial reserves of natural gas were found trapped within a layer of hard shale. Unleashing the gas had proven exceptionally difficult. The method developed in Texas and perfected by other drillers through the 1990s came to be known as the slick-water frac—it involved flushing the shale with a particular blend of water, gel, and sand to crack the rock and make it easier to draw the gas out.

There is a natural gas rush under way in Pennsylvania, and techniques like the slick-water frac are a major reason why. Pennsylvania sits atop the Marcellus shale formation, believed to hold more than 50 trillion cubic feet of accessible natural gas. The shale touches other states like New York and Ohio, but the Marcellus formation runs under almost three quarters of Pennsylvania, through the west and northern portions of the state. The gas industry maintains that new drilling and fracking techniques make these resources safely accessible. Environmental groups disagree, pointing to a blowout in Pennsylvania's Clearfield County in June 2010 and concerns over laissez-faire permitting processes by the state's Department of Conservation and Natural Resources.

Still, many folks are comfortable taking the risk. Some are down-the-line free market conservatives, but not all. Areas believed to be rich with accessible natural gas include the poorest parts of the state, and many have not seen new investment for decades. Gas leases mean big paydays for landholders in rural Pennsylvania, as well as jobs and economic development. And while the monetary benefits are one thing, there's also a psychological component—few Pennsylvanians would mind seeing the state return to its former prominence as the cradle of American energy production if it could be done in a safe, environmentally conscious way. So far, the commonwealth has taken a hands-off approach to natural gas speculation, at least relative to government involvement in neighboring states like New York. A 2009 effort to close Pennsylvania's budget gap with a tax on natural gas went nowhere. The State House in Harrisburg continues to buzz with talk about taxing gas drillers, but lawmakers are hesitant to tamper with what many see as a goose just beginning to lay golden eggs.

However one feels about the natural gas rush, there are vital lessons to draw from the state's history with the oil industry. Pennsylvania's peak oil production was more than 30 million barrels, which was pumped in 1891. Any wealth the state derived from the Pennsylvania oil rush is long gone. The boom did not last—booms never do. No matter how lucrative the Marcellus gas play is in the short term, the state's gas reserves are finite. Whatever the state decides to do should be done with an eye on the future and a plan for reinvesting gas profits locally. The Pithole Citys, Petroleum Centers, and other depopulated oil towns up and down northwest Pennsylvania are a testament to that.

Blind—a small lakefront structure designed for inconspicuous bird-watching. In addition to the varied waterfowl, bald eagles and red-tailed hawks have been known to populate the refuge. A 3-mile hike along Deer Run Trail hints at the area's robust white-tailed deer population, though you'll also find turtles and toads. Amphibians and mammals scamper throughout the refuge, sometimes right along the roadbed. Just be sure to wear insect repellent in the muggy summer months, as mosquitoes can be brutal around the marsh.

The drive takes on a new character near the small borough of **Cochranton,** where the road meets French Creek (a sizable tributary of the Allegheny River). Cochranton is also close to the end of Crawford County, an unofficial dividing line between the Pennsylvania oil region and what's commonly presented as the Pittsburgh countryside. This western-central expanse is awash in agriculture—flatter and more readily farmable than the Laurel Highlands, which border Pittsburgh from a similar distance southeast of the city.

Cross into Mercer County and look for roadside horse farms. Keep your eyes open for woodchucks as well; these furry little mammals are all over the county but have a confounding, un-Darwinian instinct for hanging around state highways. When you reach the town of **Sandy Lake,** consider a short diversion into **Maurice K. Goddard State Park,** a thin hoop of lush forest that encloses 1,800-acre warm-water Lake Wilhelm. The entrance off Sandy Lake (a 145-degree right turn) is a smooth paved road that soon turns to gravel. This entrance to the long, thin park runs alongside private residences and a couple places to buy bait. Fishing is a major draw here, and commonly caught varieties include largemouth bass, crappie, and perch. Sailboats and small motorboats are both welcome, and shelters for picnicking and charcoal grilling are located right next to most boat launches. An asphalt foot and bike path also loops around the lake. Do keep in mind that Goddard abuts a state game land, and hunting is also permitted in season within the park.

From here it's another 14 miles through farm country to **Grove City,** a well-maintained eight-thousand-person town known to many western Pennsylvanians and Ohioans for its outlet shopping (the mall is 4 miles west of downtown). There's a sizable business district downtown as well, jazzed up by the single-screen **Guthrie Theatre** and its glitzy marquee. A bit down the road is Grove City College, a liberal-arts school with five thousand students.

Cross into Butler County and enter **Slippery Rock.** PA 173 joins PA 108 just past the downtown shops, which cater to farmers and students at Slippery Rock University. The small business district offers a nice mix of food purveyors, specialty stores, and restaurants like **North Country Brewing Company,** which is especially popular among the university set. As with many schools in the region, Slippery Rock began as a teachers college and evolved into a multidisciplinary liberal-arts institution. The university is also the reason they call Slippery Rock the Town Known 'Round the World—sports announcers at big football schools across the country have taken to announcing Slippery Rock University football scores at halftime (a droll tradition that dates back to the 1936 football season). Slippery Rock also has a Prospect League baseball team. Games played in this collegiate summer league are a fun way to spend an afternoon or evening if you happen to be in town at the right time. The guy sitting next to you might be a major league scout; you never know.

While you're exploring Slippery Rock, take a short trip to historic **Rock Falls Park,** which is a clearly marked right turn off 173. This privately owned park sits on Slippery Rock Creek and is a unique, woodsy place for a quick stop or for camping at the park's music festivals. Swimming and relaxing in the creek is a great way to break up a hot summer day (just be careful; it gets a little rough downstream). It's also where a whisper-quiet, well-camouflaged water snake slithered across my foot and under a large boulder one spring afternoon before panic could set in.

Speaking of snakes, the trip's final leg travels through the **Jennings Environmental Center,** Pennsylvania's last remaining habitat for the eastern massasauga rattlesnake. To get there, follow 173 to the PA 8 intersection

Midstream at Rock Falls Park

and make a quick right for just 0.1 mile past the **Old Stone House** (a historic stagecoach stop, now a museum) and follow PA 528 south. The massasauga is one of only three venomous snakes found in Pennsylvania along with the copperhead and timber rattlesnake. A 0.5-mile hiking trail offers a chance to try your luck with the massasauga. Sightings are rare and bites even rarer, but do stay alert. Jennings is also unique for its 60 acres of prairie, an ecological rarity in this state made possible by clay that resides below the surface and wards off the hemlock and hardwood forests that typically take hold in passive Pennsylvania green space. Indeed, the rest of Jennings is covered with woodlands. Jennings is especially popular with plant enthusiasts and birdwatchers; you'll often find staffers leading guided walks through the prairie.

The environmental center is easily accessible off 528 and connects to **Moraine State Park.** The route makes a visually impressive passage over Lake Arthur, midway through the nearly 17,000-acre facility. Excellent for fishing (look for the boat rental concession on the lake's southern banks), the warm-water lake supports a wide species variety and is encircled by several hiking trails. Mountain biking is also a popular activity here. Emerge from the park's southern end and finish the drive in **Prospect,** a small, peaceable farm town.

IN THE AREA

Accommodations

Caboose Motel, 407 S. Perry Street, Titusville. Call 814-827-5730. Offers the rare opportunity to spend the night in a fully furnished caboose car. Located across from the main OC&T railroad station and visitors center in Titusville. Web site: www.octrr.org/caboosemotel.htm.

Attractions and Recreation

Drake Well Museum, 202 Museum Lane, Titusville. Call 814-827-2797. Open Tues.–Sun., May–Oct. Web site: www.drakewell.org.

Erie National Wildlife Refuge, 11296 Wood Duck Lane, Guys Mills. Call 814-789-3585. Web site: http://erie.fws.gov.

Guthrie Theatre, 232 S. Broad Street, Grove City. Call 724-458-9420. Web site: www.the-guthrie.com.

Jennings Environmental Center, Slippery Rock. Call 724-794-6011. Web site: www.dcnr.state.pa.us/stateparks/parks/jennings.aspx.

Maurice K. Goddard State Park, 684 Lake Wilhelm Road, Sandy Lake. Call 724-253-4833. Web site: www.dcnr.state.pa.us/stateparks/parks /mauricekgoddard.aspx.

Moraine State Park, 225 Pleasant Valley Road, Portersville. Call 724-368-8811. Web site: www.dcnr.state.pa.us/stateparks/parks/moraine.aspx.

National Transit Company Building, 206 Seneca Street, Oil City. Call 814-676-5303. Web site: www.ocartscouncil.com.

Oil Creek and Titusville Railroad, Perry Street Station, Titusville. Call 814-676-1733. Rides offered June–Oct.; call ahead for train schedule. Web site: www.octrr.org.

Oil Creek State Park, 305 State Park Road, Oil City. Call 814-676-5915. Web site: www.dcnr.state.pa.us/stateparks/parks/oilcreek.aspx.

Old Stone House, 2865 William Flynn Highway, Slippery Rock. Call 724-738-2409. Web site: www.oldstonehousepa.org.

Rock Falls Park, Slippery Rock. Call 724-794-2040. Web site: www.rock fallsonline.com.

Venango Museum of Art, Science and Industry, 270 Seneca Street, Oil City. Call 814-676-2007. Open Tues.–Sun., year-round. Web site: www .venangomuseum.org.

Dining and Nightlife

Blue Canoe Brewery, 113 S. Franklin Street, Titusville. Call 814-827-7181. With Bronco's Barbeque a distant memory, the Blue Canoe is now the best restaurant in Titusville. Seven beers made on-site, pizza specialties, and big sandwiches are highlights. Web site: www.thebluecanoe brewery.com.

North Country Brewing Company, 141 S. Main Street, Slippery Rock. Call 724-794-2337. Hand-hewn wooden beams hold up the ceiling of this converted building, where the cellar was once the county morgue. It's now a microbrewery that specializes in beers and burgers; order your ground beef made from local cattle ("farm to fork") or try an elk burger for a couple bucks more. Either goes great topped with tasty peppercorn bacon. Open for lunch and dinner. Web site: www.northcountrybrewing.com.

Other Contacts

Oil Region Alliance, 217 Elm Street, Oil City. Call 800-483-6264. Web site: www.oilregion.org.

Frank Lloyd Wright's famed Fallingwater Courtesy of the Western Pennsylvania Conservancy

CHAPTER

10

Laurel Highlands

Estimated length: 55 miles
Estimated time: 1–2 days

Getting there: Beginning in Somerset (exit off I-76), head west on PA 31 to Jones Mills. Take PA 711/381 south from Jones Mills to Farmington, then US 40 west to Uniontown.

Highlights: The Alleghenies don't get any steeper than this in Pennsylvania. The Highlands' back roads flirt with 3,000-foot elevations as they connect landmarks like Frank Lloyd Wright's celebrated Fallingwater with the rush of the Youghigheny River at Ohiopyle State Park. This trip also includes stops at the Fort Necessity Battleground and Laurel Caverns.

Prepare for a lot of downshifting. Between the rolling farmlands and the swell of the Allegheny Mountains, this loop through the back roads of Pennsylvania's Laurel Highlands feels like a roller-coaster ride without the tracks. Named for the 70-mile-long Laurel Mountain, the area is just to the southeast of Pittsburgh and is home to beauty both natural and man-made. The area is south of both I-76 and the Lincoln Highway, and many of the smaller roads that traverse through here are officially designated Pennsylvania scenic byways, for good reason. The high rise of the mountains allows the area to enjoy generally cooler weather than the rest of the state, making it a perfect escape from summer heat. Small inns and bed & breakfasts, old churches with worn gardens of headstones, and endless fields of corn are interspersed between the walls of thick Allegheny forestry.

Commence in **Somerset,** seat to the county of the same name. The courthouse is among the more impressive buildings in the region—a large, beaux-arts-style limestone building capped by a copper dome modeled after St. Paul's Cathedral in London. The county itself owes its name to England as well. Somerset was originally settled in 1787 but took off after bituminous coal discoveries complemented maple syrup production as a reliable revenue generator. Stop for a bite at the 50-year-old Summit Diner, easy to recognize by its neon arrow sign out front. Four miles north of the central business district (follow PA 601 to PA 985) is the **Somerset Historical Center,** a museum and outdoor interpretive center that explores farm life around the Laurel Highlands region. Learn the ins and outs of stone cutting, cabin assembly, weaving, and cider making, or just enjoy a walk around the pastoral setting. The site includes several re-created and restored homestead buildings as well as the Walter's Mill Covered Bridge, an original structure dating back to 1859.

Passing through a healthy, verdant chunk of Pennsylvania's farm country, PA 31 slopes over some of the gentlest hills on this drive. Just west out of Somerset, the Glades Pike Country Store is a one-stop shop for local produce. Nearby is the **Oakhurst Tea Room** smorgasbord and Glade's Pike Winery, which offers a tasty selection of locally produced wines and snack specialties. The sunny vistas continue as the road curves farther westward past multiple state parks. The Laurel Highlands area enjoyed a great deal of attention from the Civilian Conservation Corps, and the resulting hiking trails, swimming areas, campgrounds, and cabins are among the finest park facilities in the state.

The first one is a special beauty. It's a short detour off PA 31, so turn left at the privately owned Pioneer Park Campground site and continue 2 miles to 3,900-acre **Laurel Hill State Park.** This beautifully designed recreational gem includes 12 miles of hiking trails and 63-acre Laurel Hill Lake, where well-maintained pavilion and picnicking space overlooks kayakers and sunbathers relaxing on a sand beach. Laurel Hill achieves a rare triumph— hiking trails are perfectly isolated and tranquil yet easily accessible from the park's arterial road. The favored hike is Hemlock Trail, which traces a little more than a mile through old-growth hemlock forest around Laurel Hill Creek. Other trails (most are fine for novices) survey the mixed deciduous forest, which lives up to the Highlands' promise of cool breezes and shade on even the hottest summer days. Oak, poplar, and cherry trees predominate. Laurel Hill is also a great place to camp, with more than 250 sites walking distance from the lake. The park is adjacent to **Forbes State Forest,** known for its challenging cross-country skiing trails: a product of the high elevation and the region's typically sizable winter snowfall. Check out the nearby **Seven Springs Mountain Resort,** a premier Highlands skiing destination.

Just down the road is **Kooser State Park,** little sister to Laurel Hill. Two hundred and fifty acres enclose a small fishing lake and abut the state forest. A big draw at Kooser is the rustic cabin area; the nine cabins are a nice choice for overnighters and rent by the week during the summer. A trout stream and 47-site campground round things out. For those who prefer a more luxurious definition of "roughing it," **Hidden Valley Four Seasons Resort** also lies along PA 31, offering golf, fishing lakes, a wide variety of sports, and extensive spa facilities. During the winter it becomes a premier ski lodge.

The first bend in the loop comes at the small town of **Jones Mills** at the **Living Treasures Animal Park** and adjacent **Log Cabin Motel.** The park incorporates a petting zoo, pony rides, and other attractions popular with families. Leading southward, PA 711/381's noticeably steeper ups and downs are fringed with wildflowers and deep valleys. Roadside shops run the gamut from upscale antiques galleries in old clapboard churches to informal yard sales sprawled across front lawns. In the warmer months, there are a good number of farm produce stands doing business along 711, which merit at least a brief stop for a taste of locally grown peaches and apples. Following 711 south leads to the fittingly ordinary town of **Normalville,** where the road follows PA 381 south toward the village of **Mill Run.** Campgrounds and bed & breakfasts are sprinkled along this stretch of road, including the family-friendly **Jellystone Park.** You'll also pass Bear Run Nature Reserve, a privately operated trail network known for its gentle streams and second-growth forest.

But people don't come here just here for the natural scenery. Tucked alongside this section of PA 381 is world-famous **Fallingwater,** the crown jewel in Frank Lloyd Wright's architectural portfolio. The commission came in 1934 from Pittsburgh department store magnate Edgar Kaufmann Sr., who had been summering in a Laurel Highlands cabin for years prior but decided the time had come for more comfortable accommodations. Kaufmann asked Wright to build him a modern summer home on a secluded plot of land adjacent to Bear Run, a stream of the Youghiogheny River. But Wright fell in love with the site and decided it required something more ambitious. The design he returned to Kaufmann called for a dramatic three-story house embedded in the hillside, with sandstone slab terraces that hang delicately over the Bear Run waterfall. Wright wanted the house to feel like a natural extension of its surroundings. Ahead of his time in this regard, Wright used local materials and integrated Fallingwater seamlessly into the natural topography.

It doesn't take a doctorate in architecture to understand what's so extraordinary about Fallingwater (though Kaufmann's son Edgar Jr. earned one anyway). Visitors who are passively acquainted with the building's exterior will be delighted to discover the care the architect and his patrons applied to the little things on the inside. Wright's innovative cantilever design is replicated throughout the interior of the house, where black walnut drawers and tables slide gracefully into the walls. The floors are slicked with wax to mimic shimmering water. Windows are either fitted seamlessly into the stone columns or edged by Cherokee red frames—Wright's signature color, and a logical fit for this rustic retreat.

Edgar Jr. donated the house to the Western Pennsylvania Conservancy (WPC) in 1963, and more than 4 million people have visited since then. The site is open six days a week year-round, except for weekdays in December and all of January and February. It is most crowded in the autumn, but the cool breezes wafting off the stream and up to the terraces make even the muggiest summer day a pleasant experience. Understandably, the Kaufmanns spent as much time here as they could. Fallingwater is a little expensive—$18 for admission to the grounds and a 60- to 75-minute house tour. But it is a unique place and is not to be missed. The WPC has elected to offer exclusive overnight stays to guests willing to fork over $1,200 for the privilege, so consider the house tour a relative bargain.

A few miles down the road from Fallingwater is another treasure in **Ohiopyle State Park.** A sportsman's wonderland, the park is set against the small town of **Ohiopyle** on the banks of the Youghigheny River, which is known locally as the Yough (counterintuitively rhymes with *clock*). The river gorge spans 14 miles through the 19,052 acres of park lands and is renowned for white-water rafting—the modern name Ohiopyle comes from the native Monogahela word *ohiopehhla,* meaning "white, frothy water." Although the area was traversed by George Washington and his troops during the French and Indian War, the first white settlers did not arrive to Ohiopyle until 1794, a good 40 years later. Tourism came with the advent of the railroads in 1880, when a train ride from Pittsburgh to Ohiopyle and back cost a dollar. These days, the lands are owned by the commonwealth, with the small riverside borough of Ohiopyle serving as the hub of activity. Numerous companies offer rafting and kayaking lessons and tours on the river, which lives up to the town's name with Class III and IV rapids on the lower part of the Yough. The middle section, located near the town and the park's main access point, features slower rapids. A 27-mile crushed limestone bike trail runs along the old railroad tracks through the park and is a mostly flat, easy ride. It makes up a segment of the much longer Great Allegheny Passage trail, which covers 132 miles from McKeesport, Pennsylvania, to Cumberland, Maryland.

Ohiopyle also bookends the southern end of the famed **Laurel Highlands Trail.** This 70-mile hike follows a spectacularly scenic elevated route between two rivers: the Youghigheny at Ohiopyle and the Conemaugh River near Johnstown in the north. It runs through a nice section of **Laurel Ridge State Park** and is the preeminent way to experience Laurel Mountain. While it's a high-altitude, difficult trail, reaching elevations of 2,950 feet, the trail-heads are already close to 0.25 mile above sea level, so getting up there is at least achievable. The diversity of forests along the ridge is a main attraction; you'll see hemlock, oak, and beech-maple among new growth species like crabapple and black locust. This is owed to the various microclimates that exist along the way, stemming from the mountain's topography as well as the generational lag between the lumbering that devastated these forests in the 19th century and the reseeding that followed. There are several camping areas on the trail (reservations required), and the blazes are clear and consistent. You won't be alone up there—the Laurel Highlands Trail is understandably popular. For more information on either the Highlands trail or the Great Allegheny Passage, consult the knowledgeable staff in the **Laurel Highlands Information Center**—conveniently located across the street from the middle Yough in the town's former train station.

Back in Ohiopyle by the picturesque river, the weekend crowds can be found taking in the park's many scenic waterfalls and sliding along the natural water slides at Meadow Run. Up the hill into Ohiopyle proper, you'll find a mix of coffee shops, cafés, and ice cream parlors, as well as opportunities to rent a bike, kayak, or raft. Unlike many Pennsylvania state parks, Ohiopyle is not a well-kept secret. On summer weekends in particular, the parking lots overflow with cars (many bearing out of state license plates), and surplus vehicles line the residential streets. Throngs of visitors gather around the Ferncliff Natural Area peninsula to explore the sundry plant life. Cyclists and kayakers fill Ohiopyle's small cafés, munching salads on the **Fire Fly Grill** deck and sandwiches at the picnic tables outside Falls Market (which still bears the nameplate HOLT'S DEPARTMENT STORE from its former life). More casual recreationalists can be found swimming in the gorge and sunning on the riverbanks. It's a buoyant, family-friendly environment and a wonderful place to spend the day.

Just past Ohiopyle is a 2-mile detour up a tall twisting road to **Kentuck Knob,** Frank Lloyd Wright's second most famous Laurel Highlands residence. This one belonged to the Kagan family—ice cream tycoons from nearby Uniontown (the final stop on this tour) who befriended the Kaufmanns and managed to commission a Wright house of their own. The innovative residence was built 18 years after Fallingwater, by which time Wright was 86 years old. Kentuck Knob was among the architect's final private home designs, and he completed the drawings having never seen the project site. With its flagstone flooring, Carolina cyprus wood, and locally quarried sandstone built into the natural slope of the land, the residence embodies an aesthetic similar to that of Fallingwater on a more modest scale. Wright enthusiasts will observe signature touches like the low-

Fort Necessity National Battlefield, re-created in Farmington

ceilinged carport and the "compression and release" approach, which alternates unusually tight entrances and hallways with comparatively expansive spaces. He also plays with shapes, inserting hexagonal skylights into the terrace and outlining the kitchen in the same form. Such creative strokes make the 2,200-square-foot house seem a great deal larger than it really is. Tours take an hour and can be combined with a visit to the grounds' sculpture meadow and a scenic view—as fine a place as any to take in the Highlands' majesty. Now owned by an English lord (who purchased the home in 1986), it is a popular attraction, though not nearly as famous as Fallingwater. It can often be toured without advance reservations.

PA 381 meets US 40 at **Farmington.** The town marks historically significant Fort Necessity, immortalized as the **Fort Necessity National Battlefield** and operated by the national park service. This tale begins in 1753, when a young George Washington—at the time a 21-year-old British military officer—attempted to claim the Allegheny Valley for British colonials. The fertile soil and advantageous location at the forks of the Ohio River made it attractive to the Brits, but also to the Native Americans and French colonists who maintained a presence in the area. The region's Lenape Indians were especially hostile to the British colonists during this time—with the memory of the humane William Penn fading rapidly, the colonists had grown increasingly brazen about forcing the Lenape population west. Meanwhile, the French had established Fort Duquesne at present-day Pittsburgh, signaling an intention to stay. Washington, under orders from Governor George Dinwiddie of Virginia, moved toward Fort Duquesne. En route, his troops launched a surprise attack on Frenchmen camped 50 miles south of the fort. Known as the Battle of Jumonville Glen, this attack ended with the death of a prominent French Canadian captain.

The park screens a video dramatizing two versions of Washington's move. The French maintained that the British fired first. Washington claimed the opposite. Either way, it triggered the French and Indian War. After his sneak attack, Washington hastily constructed Fort Necessity at the battlefield's present-day site along US 40. A month later the French counterattacked and Washington got pummeled, surrendering Fort Necessity and allowing the French to keep their toehold in western Pennsylvania. It marked the beginning of a long war that emerged as a key theater of a worldwide contest between European coalitions. The American battles filled many years but ultimately resulted in the British pushing their French opposition westward, solidifying British control over Canada and the colonies.

Both the fort's interpretive center and the Mount Washington Tavern (a restored coach stop) just up the hill are interesting, informative, and well maintained. The replicated fort is minimalist by design. Five miles of hiking trails guide visitors around the park's dense forests and reconstructed historical sites. A little bit up the road is **Braddock's Grave,** memorializing the British general who led an ill-fated expedition to Fort Duquesne a year into the French and Indian War. Braddock had intended to confront what had become a French stronghold but was attacked by French and Indian combatants along the way, derailing the mission and resulting in Braddock's death.

A mix of antiques stores, farm stands, and local wineries line US 40, along with several historic inns and taverns still in business. The turnaround point at the mountaintop **Summit Inn Resort** is the best place to take in the spectacular valley view to the west, not to mention a great place to stop for lunch on the veranda. Next door to the Summit is a side road that runs past Forbes State Forest 5 miles into **Laurel Caverns,** the largest cave in Pennsylvania, with more than 3 miles of underground passages. Stop in and take the one-hour-long family tour, which is a more polished, theatrical experience than you'll get at other Pennsylvania caverns. In addition to the tight spaces, cool temperatures, and unique stone formations, the tour includes bells and whistles like a light and sound show. Above ground is a large gift shop and geologically themed miniature golf course.

US 40 dips a bit as it approaches **Uniontown.** If you time it right, you might catch a nice sunset. Uniontown is the county seat of Fayette County and was founded on July 4, 1776. Uniontown is also the birthplace of Gen.

WASHINGTON'S RETURN TO WESTERN PENNSYLVANIA

George Washington's battle at Fort Necessity in the 1750s would not be his last visit to the Laurel Highlands. He'd return 40 years later as the first American president to monitor the federal response to the Whiskey Rebellion—a populist uprising led by western Pennsylvania distillers and farmers who felt unfairly targeted by a recently implemented excise tax on whiskey. Washington, who personally opposed the tax, viewed its orderly enforcement as a test of the integrity of the new government. They reenact the rebellion every September in the Somerset County town of Berlin, where Washington's federal troops assembled and confronted the uprising. It's a reminder of the mindset that undergirded America's early, uncertain years in frontier regions like western Pennsylvania.

George C. Marshall, best known as Harry Truman's secretary of state and the man who rebuilt Europe after World War II. Universally admired American heroes like Marshall are few and far between, so Uniontown is decidedly not shy about reminding visitors of his local roots. The general's likeness is found everywhere—note the statue at the intersection of Fayette and Main streets and a large mural likening Uniontown's redevelopment program to the original Marshall Plan. The task at hand might not be as daunting, but the results have been impressive. A nice variety of shops line the Main Street business district, and the wonderfully restored **State Theatre** hosts classic musicals. I've enjoyed eating at **Meloni's** Italian restaurant on Main.

IN THE AREA

Accommodations

Hidden Valley Four Seasons Resort, 1 Craighead Drive, Hidden Valley. Call 814-443-8000. Most popular with skiing enthusiasts but suitable for all. Offers a wide variety of accommodations, from standard hotel rooms to multifloor townhouse rentals. Web site: www.hiddenvalleyresort.com.

Jellystone Park, 839 Mill Run Road, Mill Run. Call 724-455-9644. The western Pennsylvania branch of the popular family campground. Web site: www.jellystonemillrun.com.

Log Cabin Motel, 288 State Route 711, Jones Mills. Call 724-593-8200. Made with white pine wood, this 34-room motel boasts a diverse stock of rooms that run the gamut from standard doubles to multiroom suites complete with billiard tables and hot tubs. The motel is adjacent to the Living Treasures Animal Park. Web site: www.logcabinmotel.com.

Seven Springs Mountain Resort, 777 Waterwheel Drive, Seven Springs. Call 814-352-7777. A positively enormous resort campus that incorporates more than 400 hotel rooms, 32 ski slopes and trails, a golf course, spa, alpine slide, 11 restaurants, and much more. Look for packages that include your preferred recreational activities. Web site: www.7springs.com.

Summit Inn Resort, 101 Skyline Drive, Farmington. Call 1-800-433-8594. High above the steep descent into Uniontown is this hundred-year-old 94-room inn, which has played host to the likes of Warren G. Harding and Harry Truman. Old menus and advertisements displayed throughout the ground-floor lobby are complemented by the original Arts and Crafts–style furniture. Drink or dine on the sprawling front porch and take in the spectacular view. Web site: www.summitinnresort.com.

Attractions and Recreation

Fallingwater, 1491 Mill Road, Mill Run. Call 724-329-8501. Open Thurs.–Tues., Mar.–Nov.; Fri.–Sun. in Dec. Closed Jan. and Feb. Reservations highly recommended; call for tour information. Web site: www .fallingwater.org.

Forbes State Forest, 1291 Route 30 (district office), Laughlintown. Call 724-238-1200. Web site: www.dcnr.state.pa.us/forestry/stateforests /forbes/index.htm.

Fort Necessity National Battlefield, 1 Washington Parkway, Farmington. Call 724-329-5512. Open daily, year-round. Web site: www.nps.gov /fone.

Kentuck Knob, 723 Kentuck Road, Chalk Hill. Call 724-329-1901. Open year-round; call for tour information. Web site: www.kentuckknob.com.

Kooser State Park, 943 Glades Pike, Somerset. Call 814-445-8673. Web site: www.dcnr.state.pa.us/stateparks/parks/kooser.aspx.

Laurel Caverns, 2 Skyline Drive, Farmington. Call 724-438-3003. Open daily, May–Oct.; weekends in Apr. and Nov. Web site: www.laurelcaverns .com.

Laurel Highlands Trail, www.dcnr.state.pa.us/forestry/hiking/laurel .aspx.

Laurel Hill State Park, 1454 Laurel Hill Park Road, Somerset. Call 814-445-7725. Web site: www.dcnr.state.pa.us/stateparks/parks/laurelhill.aspx.

Laurel Ridge State Park, 1117 Jim Mountain Road, Rockwood. Call 724-455-3744. Web site: www.dcnr.state.pa.us/stateparks/parks/laurel ridge.aspx.

Living Treasures Animal Park, 288 PA 711, Jones Mills. Call 724-593-8300. Web site: www.ltanimalpark.com.

Ohiopyle State Park, 7 Sheridan Street, Ohiopyle. Call 724-329-8591. Web site: www.dcnr.state.pa.us/stateparks/parks/ohiopyle.aspx.

Somerset Historical Center, 10649 Somerset Pike, Somerset. Call 814-445-6077. Open Tues.–Sat., year-round. Web site: www.somersethistorical center.org.

State Theatre, 27 E. Main Street, Uniontown. Call 724-439-1360. Web site: www.statetheatre.info.

Dining and Nightlife

Fire Fly Grill, 25 Sherman Street, Ohiopyle. Call 724-329-7155. Casual spot for sandwiches, wraps, and other ways to refuel during a day spent recreating in Ohiopyle. Web site: www.thefireflygrill.com.

Meloni's, 105 W. Main Street, Uniontown. Call 724-437-2061. Unpretentious, tasty Italian preparations at one of Uniontown's oldest restaurants. Big plates of pasta and blue plate dinner specials for less than 10 dollars are the highlights. Open for lunch and dinner. Web site: www.melonis restaurant.com.

Oakhurst Tea Room, 2409 Glades Pike, Somerset. Call 814-443-2897. An all-you-can-eat smorgasbord of American comfort foods. Open for lunch, dinner, and Sun. brunch. Web site: www.oakhursttearoom.com.

Other Contacts

Laurel Highlands Visitors Bureau, 120 E. Main Street, Ligonier. Call 724-238-5661. Web site: www.laurelhighlands.org.

Looking up the Johnstown Inclined Plane

CHAPTER

11

Johnstown and the Old Allegheny Portage

Estimated length: 60 miles
Estimated time: 1 day

Getting there: Beginning in Ligonier, take PA 711 north for 2.5 miles. Merge onto PA 271 and drive north into Johnstown. After exploring Johnstown, take PA 56 east to the US 219 expressway. Continue on 219 north past the flood memorial and exit onto PA 53 north. Follow this route to the US 22 east expressway—exit at the Allegheny Portage Railroad National Historic Site and return to US 22 east after visiting. Follow US 22 into Hollidaysburg, where the drive concludes.

Highlights: This drive through the southwest is centered around Johnstown, which is a little rough around the edges but is a looking glass into the development of the state's steel economy. The welcoming small towns of Ligonier and Hollidaysburg bookend the route. Be warned that portions of this drive involve high-speed expressways, necessitated by the location of the Johnstown National Flood Memorial and the Allegheny Portage Railroad.

The hardscrabble Pennsylvania steel town is a powerful American icon. As with coal and the railroads, Pennsylvania's 19th-century steel boom meant jobs for hundreds of thousands of immigrants—English, German, Welsh, and Irish at first, and Italian and eastern European soon after. They endured hazardous conditions and long workweeks, accepting such risks and inconveniences as the price of American citizenship.

The steel boom sprouted from the state's advantageous location and its coalfields; readily accessible coal made it simple to fire the iron furnaces that dominated the state's manufacturing base prior to the Civil War. Visiting Europe in 1872, Pittsburgh businessman Andrew Carnegie toured the British steelworks owned by Henry Bessemer and left impressed with how inexpensively his mill converted pig iron into durable steel. Carnegie returned to Pennsylvania determined to transform the face of industry statewide.

Like all the wealthy industrialists of his era, Carnegie combined a good idea with a sharp understanding of markets and willingness to exploit them mercilessly. He recognized that steel would be vital to America's growth as it transitioned away from its roots in farming and textiles into a manufacturing powerhouse. His early attempts to raise the necessary capital for a state-of-the-art steelworks met some resistance, as American steel was considered basically inferior to the European product. Among the skeptics was Carnegie's old boss, Pennsylvania Railroad president John Edgar Thomson, who only reluctantly allowed the Scotch Devil (as Carnegie was known) to name his new steelworks the Edgar Thomson Steel Company in tribute. The problem was exacerbated by economic reality—the financial panic of 1873 tightened credit markets and delayed the mill's opening. But once the Edgar Thomson Steel Company was up and running, Carnegie played the market masterfully. He rolled high-quality steel, undercutting competitors' prices one day and then price fixing with the steel cartel the next. Carnegie rapidly built an empire, swallowing rival companies and entering into lucrative partnerships with the leaders of correlated industries like coke producer Henry Frick. In 1901 he sold the company and devoted the rest of his life to philanthropy. Carnegie Steel was worth more than $4 billion in today's dollars, and Pennsylvania produced 60 percent of all the steel made in America.

Steel retains a special place in Pennsylvanians' hearts and legal statutes; to this day, all state-funded capital projects in Pennsylvania are required to use domestically milled steel product. But protecting the local industry has proven extraordinarily difficult, and steel towns from the southwest to the northeast have had to find ways to cope. Pittsburgh has adjusted relatively well thanks to its size advantage. The city's jobs base includes health care services, large universities, and food production, and this built-in economic diversity has softened the blow somewhat. Smaller cities have done what they can to innovate. Bethlehem, in the Lehigh Valley, converted its colossal steel mills into a casino resort—truly a sight to behold. To me, the state's most interesting case is **Johnstown,** a 24,000-person city in the southwest corner of Cambria County and the hub of this scenic drive.

First and foremost, Johnstown is interesting in a visual sense. The *New Republic*'s Jason Zengerle describes it accurately as "surrounded on all sides by mountains, as if the city had been dropped from the sky and landed with such force that it punched a giant crater in the Alleghenies." Indeed, Johnstown seems to have been scooped out from the landscape. This geography has contributed to the city's isolation as well as its greatest tragedy. The May 31, 1889, Johnstown Flood—in which more than two thousand people were killed by the crumbling of a poorly maintained dam at an elite fishing and hunting club 14 miles upriver—is woven through the city's consciousness. There have been two major floods since then, and local attractions include a flood museum downtown and a flood memorial/historic site on the city's outskirts. Resilience in the face of adversity is a theme here. The flooding is one aspect. The economy is another.

For years, Johnstown's major employer was the Cambria Iron Works. Founded in 1852, Cambria rolled America's first domestically produced steel rails 15 years later. Its fabrication technique was conceived and patented by Pittsburgh metallurgist William Kelly, who sold his patent to Bessemer during a personal bankruptcy. Bessemer had patented his method autonomously in Great Britain, though there exists some historical controversy over which inventor really deserves the credit. Either way, history has bestowed far greater recognition on the Brit.

Cambria Iron Works predated Carnegie's introduction to the steel business, and Carnegie piggybacked on advances that had begun years earlier in Johnstown. Carnegie's first superintendent was from Cambria, as were many of the Edgar Thomson Company's original steelworkers. In the years that followed, Cambria faced numerous uphill battles; it had to compete with the increased efficiency from newer mills (such as Carnegie's) as well as recovery from the 1889 flood. Nonetheless, Cambria continued to be a highly productive facility and the bedrock of the Johnstown economy through most of the 20th century. In the 1920s Cambria was folded into Bethlehem Steel, which managed the mills through the industry's post–World War II peak and its subsequent decline. Bethlehem's Johnstown operation went dark in 1992 and compelled the city to explore its options in a poststeel era.

Significant help came from Washington, D.C., in the form of Johnstown's late congressman John Murtha. Representative Murtha grew famous for keeping the spigot of federal money turned up all the way, steering public works projects and defense contractors into his hometown with great zeal. Love him or hate him, Murtha was from the old school—a "big side of beef of a guy" (in the words of humorist P. J. O'Rourke) and unrepentant about bringing federal largesse to Johnstown. Murtha passed away in February 2010. Some have written the town's eulogy as well, though personally I find a good deal to recommend. While its struggles are easy enough to see and understand, its communities, history, architecture, and a couple one-of-a-kind attractions make Johnstown an excellent focal point for a back roads drive around southwest Pennsylvania.

As with the prior route, expect ups and downs—there's no way around it given the region's topography. The drive begins in the charming small town of **Ligonier,** to the southeast of Pittsburgh. Well cared for and compact, with a green town square and a bevy of antiques shops and cafés, Ligonier's claim to fame is its namesake, **Fort Ligonier**—a British stronghold built in 1758 to help protect Pittsburgh and house troops during the French and Indian War. Though the fort was decommissioned eight years later, visitors today can tour the 8 acres of reconstructed buildings and a well-executed museum that gamely explains the complicated subject matter. In addition to displaying rare artifacts like George Washington's saddle pistols and some original Washington writings, the museum explores the global aspect to the Seven Years War (Winston Churchill labeled it the first world war), of which the French and Indian theater in colonial America was only a part.

The fort is an easy downhill walk south from the center of town, where interested shoppers can find plenty of opportunities to pick up antiques, jewelry, used books, high-quality sportswear, and local handicrafts, as well as a bite to eat in one of a few coffee shops. Most stores stay open until 7 on Thursday, and a popular summer concert series program draws the whole village to the town square on Sunday nights. Nearby attractions include **Idlewild Park,** the oldest amusement park in Pennsylvania and

A summer concert in charming Ligonier

host of the Ligonier Highland Games every September. And Ligonier sits adjacent to the famed Lincoln Highway (US 30). Not too far from downtown on US 30 is **Ligonier Beach,** a large public pool, and a bar/restaurant.

Drive only 2.5 miles north from Ligonier, and stay right at the fork to continue along PA 271 north where the Sheetz gas station splits the road. The drive along PA 271 is essentially a straight vertical climb punctuated by 2,700-foot-high Laurel Hill Summit, and then a graduated descent through Johnstown's leafy suburbs into the central city. On the way up you'll pass over Mill Creek, alongside soccer fields and eventually the Community Arts Center of Cambria County, where gallery space for local artists complements classes and special events.

Johnstown, cradle of the steel industry

Look for the arts center on your right as you descend toward John-stown. A short distance past the center is a left turn that will lead you to the top of the **Johnstown Inclined Plane** (follow the clearly marked signs), which is in the suburban town of **Southmont.** The bright red cars are linked by steel cable and work together to move each other—as one car slides down the mountainside, the other is drawn up. This is the steepest inclined plane in the world, constructed in 1891 after the flood as a way to evacuate residents from the city during emergencies. It soon became a pop-ular commuter system for suburbanites living on the rim that encircles the city and is the area's most distinctive attraction. The spectacular views of the valley below perfectly convey Johnstown's unusual geography and the Highlands' natural splendor. Ride the inclined plane and see for yourself; a round-trip costs $4 and can be taken either top to bottom or bottom to top. Spend a few moments browsing the gift shop and visitors center at the Southmont point and consider dining at the **City View Bar & Grill,** which overlooks the valley. If you prefer, a little farther down PA 271 is the Johnstown Brewing Company.

The entrance to Johnstown proper is marked by the Chapin Arch, a stone roadside structure that was moved to this location by a former general manager of the Cambria Iron Company to memorialize his deceased wife. The sloped road passes this and then a row of frame hillside houses that typify the city's residential clusters. More ornate stone buildings can be found downtown and in the Cambria City neighborhood—a 30-block sliver of land that sits west of the Conemaugh River in the city's northwest section. Johnstown's immigrant diversity engendered all varieties of churches—German, Irish, Hungarian, Polish, Slovak, and others—many of which still stand today and constitute the city's most remarkable historic sites. After the 1889 flood leveled Johnstown, a building boom followed, and churches were the vanguard of the town's new look. As one example, the Italianate-style St. John Gualbert Cathedral downtown was among the first postflood structures in Johnstown to utilize structural steel.

Downtown also has nonecclesiastical notables. The **Johnstown Flood Museum** is the best known, occupying an old library that Andrew Carnegie built for Johnstown after the flood. It was among the first of the many American libraries he would build, though he undoubtedly felt uniquely responsible for this one since he held membership at the South Fork Fishing and Hunting Club, which owned the faulty dam. His contributions to rebuilding Johnstown were indicative of the man's complex relationship to the masses. Writer Peter Krass calls him "a flawed Shakespearean protagonist—a Macbeth, a King Lear, a Prospero." Carnegie was capable of both heavy-handed labor practices and great philanthropy; an improvement, to be sure, over the era's more punitive robber barons who lacked his empathy.

Then again, visiting the flood museum is sure to rouse anger at the mentality of the South Fork club members (whose ranks included coke titan Henry Clay Frick and financier Andrew Mellon) and their basic indifference toward the Johnstown citizenry. It was no secret that their South

Fork dam was a tenuous structure, nor that its collapse would unleash the contents of Lake Conemaugh and with it unspeakable damage on the city below.

The museum's main floor is centered around a three-dimensional model displaying the route that the flood followed, from the dam in South Fork along the Little Conemaugh River and through the valley at 40 miles per hour. The resulting damage was a dystopian nightmare of dead bodies, orphaned children, and a devastated city of smoking debris. A wall lists the people left dead by the flood (more than 2,200 in total); other exhibits cover the relief effort and the unsuccessful attempt to extract damages from the South Fork Fishing and Hunting Club. The museum's second floor is a theater that screens Charles Guggenheim's Academy Award–winning documentary about the disaster. There's also some fine material about the resilience of Johnstown and its history with the Cambria Iron Company, which employed seven thousand Johnstown residents at the time of the flood. That number doubled by 1940 after the takeover by Bethlehem and the rapid growth of the American steel industry.

Central Johnstown features some notable restaurants and stores (look for George's Song Shop, which lays claim to being the oldest record store in the United States). Do prepare for a fair number of boarded-up storefronts and derelict industrial space. If time allows, I recommend at least a short tour around Cambria City, which is an easy detour from central Johnstown west on PA 56. Pick up a walking tour at the flood museum if you're interested in identifying the various churches and civic buildings. There's also sublime fried chicken at **Our Sons Family Restaurant,** served to go or at diner-style booths. Cambria City is bounded by Broad Street, where the city's other major attractions are located. The big one is the **Heritage Discovery Center,** an interactive museum focused on the immigrant experience in the region. It offers a wide-ranging look into the challenges faced by immigrants in the industrial era as well as unusual opportunities, like the chance to practice separating faux coal from faux slate. The center also has a children's museum and rooftop garden. Next door, the **Wagner-Ritter House and Garden** is a window into the lives of Johnstown steelworkers.

When you're done with Johnstown, locate PA 56 east out of the city. Regrettably, the back roads out of Johnstown are confusing and difficult to navigate. Enterprising types may consider purchasing a map and tracking

Unger House at the Johnstown National Flood Memorial

the PA Heritage Route signs or designing their own itinerary. If you wish to follow the drive as outlined, fair warning: PA 56 out of Johnstown is an expressway, as is US 219, which should be taken north at the intersection with the PA 56 bypass. The good news is that the distance on these roads is short and scenic. Along 219 is also the exit for the **Johnstown Flood National Memorial,** which is the second site dedicated to the historic flood. The material is similar, but you're getting a different geographic perspective—the national park site is located high in the mountains close to the South Fork club where the dam broke. Exhibits incorporate recorded testimonials from flood survivors. The restored Unger House is also located here, which is where the club's manager lived. Poor Elias J. Unger did his best to patch the dam the day of the torrential rains but could do only so much.

Turn off US 219 at the PA 53 exit and drive north on this scenic back road through **Summerhill** and **Whitmore.** This segment of the route dances around the Little Conemaugh River and through two single-lane tunnels (be alert and yield to oncoming traffic). The largest town on this leg is **Portage,** a 2,800-person village that has its roots in bituminous coal mining and as a satellite town for the **Allegheny Portage Railroad.** This crucial bit of Pennsylvania history is memorialized with a national park site 9 miles later in the drive. Follow PA 53 as it twists its way through **Lilly,** merge onto US 22 eastward, and take the Gallitzin exit, which deposits you at the railroad's park site.

Inside Lemon House

The portage railroad is dually interesting—first as a technological feat and second as a snapshot into the state's development at the dawn of the industrial revolution. Determined to preserve Pennsylvania's relevance as a venue for transport, the state legislature authorized the Main Line of Public Works in 1826. This hybrid system utilized canals and railroads to move passengers, goods, and raw materials from Pittsburgh to Philadelphia and vice versa. Its main beneficiary was the Philadelphia port, which was battling increasingly robust competition from New York and Baltimore.

In attempting to move anything across Pennsylvania, engineers confronted the same challenge as the Native Americans and colonists before—the 0.5-mile-high Alleghenies. Canals could not scale the steep ridge, and railroad technology was still too primitive in 1830 to cover the full distance across the mountains. The solution—the Allegheny Portage Railroad—was an innovative coupling of canal and railroad technology. Goods and passengers were transferred from canal boats to railroad cars and lifted up a series of inclined planes across the slopes of the mountains. The cargo rejoined the canal system on the other side. Ultimately, the portage railroad helped cut the travel time across the state by 500 percent and paved the way for the Horseshoe Curve and the railroad-only system completed in 1854 (see chapter 13). It also did much to boost economic development in hub towns along the planes, namely presteel Johnstown in the west and Hollidaysburg in the east.

The portage railroad held the keys to Pennsylvania's prosperity for about 20 years. This period is memorialized at the railroad's national park site. The railroad was completely disassembled long ago, so the piece of track and engine house you'll see here are reconstructions. A boardwalk takes visitors from the main center (exhibit space and a theater) to the engine house area, where you may find historical interpreters putting on stonecutting demonstrations or other exhibitions. There's an original structure here as well—the sandstone Lemon House, an 1832 inn that served the visitors and portage railroad workers who traveled and worked along the planes.

After the railroad site, return to US 22 east toward Hollidaysburg. This final expressway segment is an elevated route. Look out the driver's side window and see if you can spot trains winding their way through the Alleghenies. Stay on 22 as it changes from expressway to local road and follow through **Duncanville,** which is home to the cavernous Antique

Blair County Jail in Hollidaysburg. Note the pillars of Chimney Rocks Park in the distance.

Depot flea market. One highlight here is the 6,000 square feet devoted to furniture sales.

The drive concludes in the hometown of steel's most whimsical application—the Slinky. In addition to serving as the reentry point for the canal system in the days of the portage railroad, **Hollidaysburg** is where Slinkys have been manufactured since 1964. Don't expect too much Slinky-related kitsch, though; Hollidaysburg is content to remain a quiet, friendly, and handsome small town with a large historic district. You'll find a fair share of curio and gift shops, bed & breakfasts like the Victorian-style **Iron Corbel**

Inn, as well as tea rooms, cafés, and coffeehouses. A concert series of local music draws crowds in the summer.

Hollidaysburg also has a wealth of notable architecture. Rows of Greek Revival buildings and lovingly preserved Federal-style brick houses line several blocks. The showcase structures are mostly Gothic—the peach stone Blair County courthouse could almost be mistaken for a cathedral with its unusual, distinctive spire. The nearby Blair County Jail is a castle-like medieval Gothic structure that will evoke Eastern State Penitentiary in the minds of Philadelphians. Though much smaller, the Blair County facility is still operational. While examining the jail, look off into the distant mountains facing south, and you'll see the Chimney Rocks. This unique Hollidaysburg landmark is a cluster of limestone pillars that stick out from the ridge. It is believed that local Native Americans used the rocks as markers and that tribal chiefs considered the spot a perfect place to keep watch over the settlement. To visit the pillars, hike up to **Chimney Rocks Park** and enjoy a terrific view from up high.

Closer to downtown, visit **Canal Basin Park,** at the site where the portage railroad met the canal that moved goods between Hollidaysburg and Columbia in Lancaster County. The park has a playground, trail, and reconstructed canal locks. The historically interesting **U.S. Hotel Restaurant & Tavern** (no longer a hotel but still a restaurant and tavern) is a short stroll away.

IN THE AREA

Accommodations

Iron Corbel Inn, 703 Allegheny Street, Hollidaysburg. Call 814-696-0324. A fine example of Hollidaysburg's superb Victorian architecture and a popular bed & breakfast. Ground-floor furnishings lend a country flavor. Web site: www.ironcorbelinn.com.

Attractions and Recreation

Allegheny Portage Railroad, 110 Federal Park Road, Gallitzin. Call 814-886-6150. Open daily, year-round. Web site: www.nps.gov/alpo.

Canal Basin Park, 101 Canal Street, Hollidaysburg. Call 814-696-4601.

Chimney Rocks Park, Chimney Rocks Road, Hollidaysburg. Call 814-695-7543.

Fort Ligonier, 200 S. Market Street, Ligonier. Call 724-238-9701. Open daily, Apr.–Nov. Web site: www.fortligonier.org.

Heritage Discovery Center, 201 Sixth Avenue, Johnstown. Call 814-539-1889. Open daily, year-round. Web site: www.jaha.org/Discovery Center.

Idlewild Park, Ligonier. Call 724-238-3666. Web site: www.idlewild.com.

Johnstown Flood Museum, 304 Washington Street, Johnstown. Call 814-539-1889. Open daily, year-round. Web site: www.jaha.org/Flood Museum.

Johnstown Flood National Memorial, 733 Lake Road, South Fork. Call 814-495-4643. Open daily, year-round. Web site: www.nps.gov/jofl.

Johnstown Inclined Plane, 711 Edgehill Drive, Johnstown. Call 814-536-1816. Open daily, year-round. Web site: www.inclinedplane.org.

Ligonier Beach, 1752 Route 30, Ligonier. Call 724-238-5553.

Wagner-Ritter House and Garden, 418 Broad Street, Johnstown. Call 814-539-1889. Open Wed.–Sun., Apr.–Oct. Web site: www.jaha.org /WagnerHouse.

Dining and Nightlife

City View Bar & Grill, 709 Edgehill Drive, Johnstown. Call 814-534-0190. The food (mostly standard American and Italian) ain't half bad, but the main attraction is the view. Tables overlook Johnstown and the valley from atop the inclined plane. Look for the excellent midweek drink specials at the bar. Open for lunch, dinner, and Sun. brunch. Web site: www .cityviewbarandgrill.com.

Our Sons Family Restaurant, 800 Broad Street, Johnstown. Call 814-536-6554. High-quality cheap eats in Cambria City.

U.S. Hotel Restaurant & Tavern, 401 S. Juniata Street, Hollidaysburg. Call 814-695-9924. This historic, restored property was built for the travelers and workers associated with the lucrative 19th-century canal economy that put Hollidaysburg on the map. It's now a dimly lit tavern and multiroom restaurant space that serves solid pub food and a wide selection of Continental entrées. Open for lunch, dinner, and Sun. brunch. Web site: www.theushotel.com.

Other Contacts

Johnstown and Cambria County Convention & Visitors Bureau, 416 Main Street, Suite 100, Johnstown. Call 814-536-7993. Web site: www.visitjohnstownpa.com.

Inside Woodward Cave

CHAPTER

12

Williamsport to State College

Estimated length: 80 miles
Estimated time: 1–2 days

Getting there: Beginning in Williamsport, drive south on PA 15 to Lewisburg. Explore its business district, switch to PA 45, and follow it west for a little more than 50 miles. At the US 322 junction, take the business route and drive west into State College.

Highlights: Competitive sports play a major role in this drive, which weaves visitors through the alternately mountainous and fertile central Pennsylvania region. The Little League World Series is played annually in Williamsport, a one-time lumber boomtown that has embraced its identification with the founding of the game. The end point at State College marks Penn State University and its football squad, a perennial contender for national champion.

There are many things that a wall map won't tell you about Pennsylvania: the beauty of Presque Isle State Park in winter, the taste of Amish root beer, and the ethereal quiet of Centralia (to name just a few). But to those who've spent any time exploring the state, a map's most glaring inadequacy is its failure to convey the challenge posed by the Allegheny Mountains. Vast and steep, the Alleghenies extend diagonally across Pennsylvania from

Rowley House, on Williamsport's Millionaires Row

the southwest through the north-central wilds like a blockade. Technology has helped us conquer these mountains, but not as much as we think. I speak from experience when I say that scaling the Alleghenies will cause an underpowered compact sedan to whine in agony. And few things are scarier to a backcountry driver than an icy, foggy day spent sliding around the two-lane roads that dip, dive, and cling to the Alleghenies' spine. Put yourself in the place of the Native Americans or the European settlers who found Pennsylvania in the 17th century, and it is small wonder that most settlements stood east of these mountains in greater Philadelphia or the flat, fertile south-central territory.

Even after a handful of minor villages sprung up along the mountainous region of central Pennsylvania, these places were held at arm's length by the rest of the state. That is, of course, until the thirst for lumber drove speculators to invest in the region and assemble the requisite commercial infrastructure. As with all booms, the lumber rush was rife with unintended consequences. One such consequence was the meteoric rise of **Williamsport**—a classic example of how geography can dictate history. Tucked in the Alleghenies, sleepy little Williamsport had just a couple hundred residents when it became the seat of Lycoming County around the turn of the 19th century. When it came time to erect a courthouse, the builders were paid in whiskey. But Williamsport also offered access to the mighty Susquehanna River, and with it, a means to transport and store all the lumber the mid-Atlantic states could ever need. Or so it was assumed.

In 1836, the West Branch Canal was completed, connecting Williamsport to Pennsylvania's main population centers. But many small towns had canal access—what made Williamsport uniquely important came a decade and a half later when sawmill owner James Perkins opened the Susquehanna Boom.

Conceptually, the boom was a simple thing. It was a section of the Susquehanna that Perkins and his partners organized into a waiting area for timber to float before it was cut into lumber—basically an unsheltered warehouse on a river. But the boom organized and professionalized the lumber industry, which was still in its early anarchic stages. Perkins paid cash for labor, helping to extinguish the inefficient and predatory barter system that had been in place during the industry's early years. He also brought order and logic to the supply chain. Lumbermen in the north-central mountains cut the pine and floated it down the Susquehanna where it was stored in the boom. A sawmill owner then purchased the logs, cut them into usable lumber, and had the product shipped by canal (and eventually by railroad) to Philadelphia, Pittsburgh, Harrisburg, York, or wherever resource-hungry industrial-era America needed it. At peak production levels, the north-central Pennsylvania forests helped supply Europe and the West Indies with lumber. The boom held up to 300 million feet of felled timber at any given time and put Williamsport and its rapidly expanding league of sawmills on the map.

Between 1850 and 1870, Williamsport was transformed from prototypical north-central Pennsylvania small town into thriving metropolis. It famously boasted more millionaires per capita than any other American city during this era. Lumber and manufacturing barons built grandiose Victorian mansions for themselves on W. Fourth Street—a portion of downtown Williamsport now known as Millionaires Row. Among these barons was Peter Herdic, a sawmill operator and president of the Susquehanna Boom, whose 411 W. Fourth Street address is now the city's most renowned bed & breakfast, the **Peter Herdic Inn.** If you would like to tour an exquisite historic Williamsport mansion without staying in one, see if you can arrange a visit to the **Rowley House.** This Queen Anne–style mansion incorporates materials from around the world, and its rare woodwork and stained glass are a peek into what it was like to be an industrial-era millionaire. Call ahead to schedule a tour.

History trolleys tour Millionaires Row in the summertime and leave from the **Peter Herdic Transportation Museum.** Walking the historic district is also an enjoyable way to spend an hour. Heading west from downtown, stop at the **Thomas Taber Museum,** a first-rate historical attraction that follows Lycoming County from the Ice Age to the present. Exhibits include life-sized dioramas of life in the region and an expectedly thorough history of the lumber industry. And there's also LaRue Shempp's extraordinary toy train collection on the basement level, which displays a lifetime's worth of collecting. Most cars are kept securely behind glass, but there are also two functioning layouts.

Another thing to like about the Taber museum is its thorough presentation of the region's social and economic history after the lumber boom. As Williamsport's fortunes grew increasingly wedded to the lumber industry, the town became a hot spot for labor unrest. Lumbermen fought management much like the anthracite miners, who were engaged in similarly dangerous and physically taxing work. But the lumber industry had a shorter trajectory than King Coal. By the time any significant labor concessions were made, the north-central forests had been mostly destroyed, and the industry was in decline.

Major efforts have been made to preserve the city's historic district, though one cannot help but notice Williamsport no longer has quite so many millionaires. With lumber on the way out, the town diversified into a more conventional manufacturing economy. Modern Williamsport is a smaller city than it once was but is clean, safe, and interesting. The 1940 WPA guide deems Williamsport "attractively laid out despite the fact that it is criss-crossed by railroads and major highways," and this remains the case. An easily walkable downtown includes a small core of office buildings, a new movie theater, clothing stores, a coffee bar, and a couple microbreweries. Lycoming College brings in a significant student population, and multiple hotel chains have locations downtown near the banks of the Susquehanna. These hotels are here for both business and leisure travelers, but also for the town's most enduring claim to fame: Little League Baseball.

To the extent that non-Pennsylvanians have ever heard of Williamsport, it is mostly in its capacity as host of the Little League World Series. The annual series is played just across the river in **South Williamsport** every August. The series features the best of the best—eight American teams and eight international teams who have won the right to play for the championship in rural Pennsylvania. The road to Williamsport is a long one, but reaching the series remains a crowning achievement for many young athletes.

Follow US 15 over the Susquehanna River into South Williamsport, and you'll find both the fields where the series is played and the **Peter J. McGovern Little League Museum.** Open weekends year-round and daily in the summer, the museum tells the story of Little League baseball in a creative, engaging way. Some exhibits are a little dated (the place opened in 1982), but kids still have fun clocking their pitching speed and practicing T-ball. Memorabilia collections include rare photographs, news clippings, and original scorecards from the league's early years. If you're here during the series, attend a game or two at the adjacent fields. Tickets are free, but if you can't get your hands on any, snag a spot on the grass overlooking Howard J. Lamade Stadium.

A bit past the Little League complex on the opposite side of US 15 is a great scenic overlook of Williamsport and the Susquehanna Valley (elevation 1,080 feet). There is no legal way to make the left, so you have to continue down the road and turn around. South of the overlook are a few notable shops, like the multidealer Bald Eagle Antique Center.

THE HISTORY OF LITTLE LEAGUE BASEBALL

While Little League baseball is now an international phenomenon, and the series is broadcast on television, the league's beginnings were humble. Playing catch with his nephews one spring day in 1938, Williamsport clerk Carl Stotz asked them how they would feel about participating in organized baseball. Stotz's original league had three teams, all named for local businesses (Lycoming Dairy, Lundy Lumber, and Jumbo Pretzel) whose sponsorship paid for uniforms and equipment. The idea caught on like wildfire, and leagues sprouted up across Pennsylvania, the United States, and eventually the entire globe.

Eight miles from South Williamsport is **Allenwood.** The highlight here is **Clyde Peeling's Reptiland,** a nifty little reptile zoo where you can get within a glass pane's separation of poisonous snakes like the black mamba, which slithers around at up to 7 miles an hour (making it the world's fastest snake) and sports an impish, guilty grin. On the opposite end of the speed spectrum are the enormous Galapagos and Aldabra tortoises, which alternate between indoor and outdoor habitats depending on the weather. Animal shows at the zoo's Program Centre are educational and offer the audience opportunities to pet a reptile or two. Shows conclude with a visit to the American alligator habitat.

The road from Allenwood through White Deer Township is the drive's least-interesting stretch. US 15 becomes an expressway for a few miles as

Howard J. Lamade Stadium, where the Little League World Series is played every August

the road bobs past I-80. Suburban-style shopping centers follow. One potentially worthwhile diversion is the Silver Moon Consignment Barn, which is an uncluttered presentation of crafts and assorted Americana. Behind the barn is an indoor-outdoor flea and farmer's market where you might find local produce.

US 15 intersects with PA 45 just outside **Lewisburg** in Union County. Rather than make the right turn on 45 to travel west (as the driving directions dictate), make the left turn and go east for less than a mile to experience the downtown first. Lewisburg is an elegant little place, distinguished by its Federal, Victorian, and Greek Revival architecture and its sidewalks lined by three-globed street lamps. Many small Pennsylvania towns have an attractive "showcase" Main Street but drab, uninteresting side blocks. Not so with Lewisburg. Its residential side streets are as uniformly picturesque as its business district.

Lewisburg's major employers include 3,500-student Bucknell University, a popular choice for matriculating undergraduates looking for a liberal arts college with a prestigious reputation, and less-than-popular Lewisburg Federal Penitentiary. Located beside Buffalo Creek, which stems from the West Branch of the Susquehanna, the town got its start as a hub for farming and textile production. Creek-side hotels were popular once but disappeared with the railroad era. Just beyond the main business corridor is the **Street of Shops**—a converted woolen mill that now functions as an indoor marketplace. The ground floor is an orderly mix of arts, crafts, prints, collectibles, and comfort food. The basement area is like a garage sale held by an atypically interesting neighborhood. I've found myself browsing down there for hours.

The three-globed street lamp is one Lewisburg symbol. The other is the bison, which serves as Bucknell's mascot. A large bison insignia crowns the art deco Campus Theatre, which also sports the school's orange and blue colors on its façade. This is a tribute to the mountain buffalo, which once roamed central Pennsylvania. If time allows, see the **Packwood House Museum,** a log-built structure turned English manor house. And look for other downtown notables like the handsome **Lewisburg Hotel** and adventuresome **Brasserie Louis** bistro.

Once you're done with Lewisburg, swing the car around and travel west on PA 45. Be on the lookout for horse-drawn buggies—there are clusters of Amish and Mennonite homesteads throughout Union County, and you'll pass several along this stretch. The Amish have been farming central Pennsylvania for centuries, but their numbers rose quickly in the second half of the 20th century, as rising land prices and expanding population in Lancaster County drew hordes of Pennsylvania Dutch westward from their oldest settlement. Many Amish and Mennonite communities have sprung up near **Mifflinburg,** a cute farming town of furniture stores and roadside barns. Good summer food abounds, from Amish produce auctions to inexpensive, quality American fare. On the borough's outskirts find **Royal Burger,** where they prepare everything fresh, from a traditional quarter-pounder to a unique Italian bruschetta burger. And it's hard to pass the Purple Cow ice cream stand without picking up a soft-serve cone.

One clue that you're among the Amish is the **Mifflinburg Buggy Museum,** which incorporates the buildings once used by coach maker William A. Heiss to manufacture horse-drawn buggies. For a short period between the arrival of railroads and the mass production of automobiles, Mifflinburg was the Detroit of carriages.

It's a short distance from Mifflinburg to **Bald Eagle State Forest,** an immense, 196,000-acre tract that crosses the border between Union and Centre counties. Named for Lenape chief Bald Eagle, the forest is also a good place to watch for the rare bird. Its hickory trees and mountain vistas extend both north and south of PA 45—how much time you want to spend exploring the forest will depend on season and personal taste. A segment of Pennsylvania's 327-mile-long Mid State Trail (MST) runs through Bald Eagle. It is a rewarding, at times harrowing, experience, and it's recommended for experienced hikers who are up for navigating a rocky trail. The hike is popular with bear enthusiasts, as the area supports a relatively robust American black bear population.

The drive offers an entry point to the Mid State Trail (with a parking area) just over the Centre County border. Back on the Union County side is the Joyce Kilmer Natural Area, a comparatively small piece of old-growth forest with its own small trail. There are many parks and forests named for Kilmer, who wrote often about his love of the natural world. His primary claim to fame was the six rhyming couplets that constituted the famous poem "Trees" (I think that I shall never see / A poem lovely as a tree...). Indeed, the trees around his natural area are quite lovely. Note the virgin white pine, spared by the 19th-century timber industry.

On the western edge of the forest is **Woodward,** best known for the **Woodward Cave.** Two miles off PA 45, the cave is an exquisite example of the unusual beauty hidden beneath central Pennsylvania. The site offers a campground and cabin rentals, but it's worth touring even if you're just passing through. Tour guides show visitors through the five-room cave— among Pennsylvania's largest—and discuss its history and science, pausing to operate the lights and giving photographers a chance to capture the cave coral and stalagmite (hint: experiment with and without the flash). The cave is packed with unique formations like the Camel, the Nittany Lion, and the Three Wise Men, which closely resemble their monikers if you use a little imagination. Fossils and hidden tunnels are among the other surprises, but keep special lookout for the sleeping bats that hang from the cave's ceiling. Woodward also boasts Pennsylvania's largest stalagmite (14 by 8 feet) and the wet Hanging Gardens Room, where you'll want to linger and explore. The cave is a cool 44 to 48 degrees year-round, so wear layers, even in the summertime.

A couple speck-sized towns interrupt the rural scenery between Woodward and the US 322 intersection. And we're now within 25 miles of Penn State University and its sizable lodging demands, so you'll start seeing bed & breakfasts sprinkled between the farms and tack shops. First up is **Aaronsburg,** which was founded by Philadelphia merchant Aaron Levy. Levy purchased the land from the commonwealth in 1783 and then deeded the six-hundred-lot town, known for its unusually wide streets, to German immigrants who inhabited the area. Next is **Millheim,** a neat little 750-person hamlet that sits on Elk Creek and draws occasional student visitors from Penn State. Millheim's tiny Main Street has a genuine find in **Elk Creek Café and Ale Works.** A couple doors down from the café sits the Wine Shop of Millheim, where multiple central Pennsylvania vineyards offer their wines. Of the eight businesses on Millheim's Main Street, two are alcohol purveyors. I like Millheim.

If you're in the mood for another cavern, there's a right turn near the town of **Spring Mills** for Penn's Cave (which is a 3-mile trip off PA 45). Those who have spent any time driving around central Pennsylvania have likely seen one of the cave's ubiquitous billboards. Visitors here are given a motorboat tour around the limestone cavern. (Note that the Woodward Cave tour mentioned earlier is a walking tour, though you'll see many of the same things here.)

Proceed onto the business route of US 322 and enter **State College,** designed from its conception to support agricultural education. What began as a humble farm school dedicated to advancing soil cultivation technology is now 44,000-student Penn State University—the system's

The State College streetscape

largest campus by far. University life and town life are virtually inseparable, as State College is powered by Penn State and Penn State is powered by State College. The stable jobs base, beautiful central Pennsylvania scenery, clean country air, small town feel, eclectic mix of restaurants, and location in the geographic center of Pennsylvania have earned State College numerous plaudits as one of America's "best" and "smartest" places to live. It's hard to disagree.

As the name implies, State College and Penn State grew together, and the school is so vast that it is almost inseparable from the town. Agricultural research done at Penn State has benefitted Pennsylvania farmers since the 1850s. This relationship has helped alleviate some of the tension that typically exists in college towns between students and locals, even if a cultural divide exists.

As anyone with a passing familiarity of collegiate athletics knows, sports are huge in State College, especially football. Longtime Penn State head coach Joe Paterno enjoys near-demigod status, with his likeness appearing on town murals and his name on a university library. Nittany Lions logo wear seems to be sold in half the stores around town. Tickets to Penn State football games can be tough to get, but just visiting the campus on game day is an experience.

There's lots of other stuff to do. The tastiest way to experience Penn State's contribution to agricultural science is a visit to the **Berkey Creamery,** a research and production facility on the north side of campus. The creamery serves sublime, fresh ice cream (just four days "from cow to cone"), and an enormous dish is only $2.75. Flavors change regularly, though standbys like Peachy Paterno are always available. You can also get ice cream, cheeses, and other dairy products to go.

While you're on campus, check out the free **Palmer Museum of Art** and the *Lion Shrine* sculpture. The school also offers overnight accommodations at the **Nittany Lion Inn.** State College has more than a dozen hotels and bed & breakfasts in and around the university, which means great off-season deals. Room rates dip during the winter and summer vacation, and peak during football weekends and graduation season. Summer is a nice time to visit, because while the town is quieter, it's hardly dead. State College boasts a variety of bars, grills, burger joints, higher-end Continental fare, and a number of quality ethnic restaurants like campus favorite **Herwig's Austrian Bistro.**

IN THE AREA

Accommodations

Lewisburg Hotel, 136 Market Street, Lewisburg. Call 570-523-7800. This attractive Victorian-style hotel in downtown Lewisburg, lavishly restored to its 19th-century splendor, is adorned with polished brass and dark woods. Hotel rooms in the original building are superior to those in the motel annex but go for twice as much per night. Web site: www.lewisburg hotel.com.

Nittany Lion Inn, 200 W. Park Avenue, State College. Call 800-233-7505. The more luxurious of Penn State's two on-campus hotels, located on the south side of campus (the Penn Slater bookends the north side). Web site: www.pshs.psu.edu/nittanylioninn.

Peter Herdic Inn, 411 W. Fourth Street, Williamsport. Call 570-326-0411. There are six distinctively designed and furnished Victorian rooms at this Millionaires Row mansion, once owned by the man who built Williamsport and revolutionized Pennsylvania's lumber economy. The inn is a superb value for the money. Web site: www.herdichouse.com.

Attractions and Recreation

Bald Eagle State Forest, 18865 Old Turnpike Road, Millmont. Call 570-922-3344. Web site: www.dcnr.state.pa.us/forestry/stateforests/baldeagle.aspx.

Clyde Peeling's Reptiland, 18628 Route 15, Allenwood. Call 570-538-1869. Open daily, year-round. Web site: www.reptiland.com.

Mifflinburg Buggy Museum, 598 Green Street, Mifflinburg. Call 570-966-1355. Open Thurs.–Sun., Apr.–Oct. Web site: www.buggymuseum.org.

Packwood House Museum, 15 N. Water Street, Lewisburg. Call 570-524-0323. Open Tues.–Sat., year-round. Web site: www.packwoodhousemuseum.com.

Palmer Museum of Art, Curtin Road, Penn State University, State College. Call 814-865-7672. Web site: www.palmermuseum.psu.edu.

Peter Herdic Transportation Museum, 810 Nichols Place, Williamsport. Call 570-601-3455. Web site: www.phtm.org.

Peter J. McGovern Little League Museum, 525 Route 15, South Williamsport. Call 570-326-3607. Open daily, June–Aug.; Fri.–Sat. only, Sept.–May. Web site: www.littleleague.org/learn/museum.htm.

Rowley House, 960 W. Third Street, Williamsport. Call 570-323-8080. Web site: www.preservationwilliamsport.org.

Street of Shops, 100 N. Water Street, Lewisburg. Call 570-524-5765. Web site: www.streetofshops.net.

Thomas Taber Museum, 858 W. Fourth Street, Williamsport. Call 570-326-3326. Open Tues.–Sat., year-round, as well as Sun., May–Oct. Web site: www.tabermuseum.org.

Woodward Cave, Woodward Cave Drive, Woodward. Call 814-349-9800. Open daily, June–Aug.; weekends, Apr.–May and Sept.–Oct. Web site: www.woodwardcave.com.

Dining and Nightlife

Berkey Creamery, 119 Food Science Building, Penn State University, State College. Call 814-865-7535. Web site: www.creamery.psu.edu.

Brasserie Louis, 101 Market Street, Lewisburg. Call 570-524-5559. Specialty beers, a wine-paired tasting menu, and creative fusion cuisine housed in an attractive lavender building in central Lewisburg. Open for lunch and dinner.

Elk Creek Café and Ale Works, 100 W. Main Street, Millheim. Call 814-349-8850. A wonderful place. They brew six beers on-site (sample them all for eight bucks) and dish up a creative, New American menu using local ingredients Wed.–Sun. It's all served in a bright, colorful dining room, which also includes a small performance space for local bands. Open for lunch (Fri.–Sat.), dinner, and Sun. brunch. Web site: www.elk creekcafe.net.

Herwig's Austrian Bistro, 132 W. College Avenue, State College. Call 814-238-0200. The menu changes daily, but expect to see top-notch Wiener schnitzel, pork sausage, and other wonderfully caloric Austrian delicacies. It's also a BYO, so get your hands on some good German beer and bring it along. Open for lunch and dinner. Web site: www.herwigs austrianbistro.com.

Royal Burger, 310 E. Chestnut Street, Mifflinburg. Call 570-966-3990. Several cuts above your average short-order burger joint in both quality and variety.

Other Contacts

Central Pennsylvania Convention and Visitors Bureau, 800 E. Park Avenue, State College. Call 814-231-1400. Web site: www.vistitpennstate .org.

Rounding the Horseshoe Curve

CHAPTER

13

Altoona North

Estimated length: 95 miles
Estimated time: 1–2 days

Getting there: Start in Altoona and drive north on PA 36 for approxi-mately 95 miles up to Cook Forest State Park. It's a mostly simple route, but make sure to look for PA 36 road signs.

Highlights: A meandering drive through a unique region, this one opens with Altoona and a side trip past the 150-year-old Horseshoe Curve. Watch the trains traverse the mountains and continue through to Gobbler's Knob in Punxsutawney. Finish the drive gazing up at the sky-high old-growth trees in Cook Forest State Park.

In 1942, eight German saboteurs were sentenced to death by an Ameri-can military tribunal. The saboteurs had intended to execute Operation Pastorius—a Nazi-devised scheme to destroy key American industrial sites and infrastructure throughout the mid-Atlantic states. After the group nar-rowly escaped an encounter with the Coast Guard on the south shore of Long Island, two of the men confessed to the FBI. Arrests were made before the plot was carried out. Domestically, news of the plan stoked wartime dis-trust and helped lead to the internment and investigation of both natural-ized and native-born German Americans.

Adolf Hitler himself had ordered the sabotage. It was the dawn of American involvement in World War II, and Nazi Germany was anxious to hobble American industry before it could regain its pre-Depression footing. While a tremendous effort was needed to defeat the Axis powers, the American industrial network was capable of staggering output. Operation Pastorius involved several targets, but the tactical priority was a 0.5-mile stretch of railroad track that spanned the Allegheny Mountains 5 miles from Altoona, Pennsylvania. It was known to most as the Horseshoe Curve, but to engineers it was known as the eighth wonder of the modern world.

Now a national historic landmark, the Curve was constructed in 1854. It was designed by none other than John Edgar Thomson, mentor to Andrew Carnegie, engineer by training, and early president of the Pennsylvania Railroad. The Curve was Thomson's answer to a difficult puzzle: how to get trains across the Allegheny Mountains quickly and safely. An initial attempt—the Allegheny Portage Railroad (see chapter 11)—was a clever solution, but it relied on a complex series of cables and several inclined planes, all of which added time and uncertainty to the process. Thomson's Curve kept the gradient to a manageable level, which allowed a steam engine to cross the Alleghenies smoothly. Its opening marked a new age for industrial America.

The Nazis were privy to what Americans had understood for close to a century: if you want to shackle American industry, stop the supply chain at the Alleghenies. The economic miracle that kept the United States humming for the better part of its industrial history was made possible by the railroads, and particularly by the link between the original colonies and the burgeoning Midwest. To fully realize the benefits of westward expansion, manufacturing states needed a fast, reliable way to obtain raw materials and move human capital. Just as important was a connection to the ports on the eastern shore. Essentially what was required was the Pennsylvania Railroad.

The story of the Pennsylvania Railroad (known as the "Pennsy" or PRR) begins more than a hundred years prior to World War II, when the northeast and mid-Atlantic states started thinking seriously about how to obtain, ship, and organize the bevy of new resources that existed throughout the Louisiana Territory. In the early 19th century, canals were the primary venue for moving raw materials and finished goods. The commonwealth almost dropped the ball in developing a canal system— throughout this period the dawdling Pennsylvania state legislature was consistently hesitant to fund the transportation network needed to modernize trade throughout the state. But New York and Washington soon forced the issue, authorizing the Erie Canal and the Chesapeake & Ohio Canal respectively. As Mike Schafer and Brian Solomon observe in *Pennsylvania Railroad,* these systems taken together posed an existential threat to Philadelphia by concentrating trade routes around New York and Baltimore.

The commonwealth eventually approved what became known as the Main Line of Public Works—a mixture of canal and railroad systems along southern Pennsylvania, ultimately intended to connect Pittsburgh to Philadelphia. But canals were already well along the way to obsolescence. In 1847, the state chartered the private Pennsylvania Railroad to create a logical, far-reaching rail system. Thomson soon became president and built the system aggressively, expanding from southern Pennsylvania across the Midwest and north to the Great Lakes. By the time the expansion ended, the network ran from easternmost Long Island as far west as St. Louis. It connected Washington to Buffalo, Chicago to Philadelphia, and everywhere in between. Originally a commercial railroad, the Pennsy soon discovered profitability in passenger rail. It cultivated an upmarket reputation, serving gourmet meals and affording passengers plush overnight accommodations. It also acquired and developed commuter systems, which had begun to take hold around old East Coast cities. Many of today's major commuter rail systems—the Long Island Railroad in New York and SEPTA's Paoli Local through the Philadelphia suburbs—were once part of the Pennsylvania Railroad. By 1920, the PRR had become among the largest, most important American corporations in history.

Of course, the Pennsy is no more, having been done in by baby-boomera mismanagement, badly conceived federal regulation, and America's schizophrenic approach to rail travel. In some sense, the PRR's downfall paralleled the decline of the state's other heavy industries. Car culture took hold with the advent of the interstate highway system, and trucks became an increasingly popular mode of commercial shipping. Still, using the traditional postwar economic trends to explain away decline are a tinge unsatisfying when it comes to the railroads. The country maintains most of the expansive rail network built by the PRR and other private carriers, with AMTRAK and regional authorities managing passenger rail. Walking around Altoona—still crisscrossed with track, rail yards, shops, and half-converted space—it is tempting to imagine a counterfactual history that was a little kinder to the Pennsy and a little kinder to her home base in the Allegheny Mountains.

If ever a single industry built a town, the railroads built **Altoona.** A staggering amount of infrastructure was required to support the Horseshoe Curve, and once it was finished, Altoona quickly became a hub for American railroading. Freight yards and repair shops served as the employment base. Reserve engines waited downtown to assist with powering passing trains over the Alleghenies. The Pennsy also set up regional offices in Altoona. A mix of German, Irish, Italian, eastern European, and Jewish immigrants formed the thriving, moderately sized city that seemed to have been built overnight. Altoona tripled in size between 1860 and 1870 as the PRR planted its roots quick and deep. At its early-20th-century peak, more than 15,000 people worked for the PRR—a quarter of Altoona's population at that time.

Geographically similar to Johnstown, Altoona is handsomer. As a general rule, railroading offered a bit more upward mobility than steelwork, which permitted a larger middle class and a more eclectic architecture to take hold. The logistical downside to Altoona's railroading history is the chaotic urban planning. Its downtown grid is sliced and diced by track, disrupted by rail yards, and on the whole pretty confusing to a nonnative. I've made wrong turns all over Pennsylvania, but never with such frequency as in Altoona.

Fortunately, the major sites are well marked. Twelfth Avenue and the surrounding blocks form the main commercial corridor, which is where you'll find the nexus of the local arts scene at the **Mishler Theatre.** A few blocks south across the famed rail yards is the **Railroaders Memorial Museum**—the town's premier attraction and an engrossing piece of history. The museum traces not only the ins and outs of railroading, it shines a spotlight on Altoona's development and how the Pennsy made it possible. Exhibits occupy the second and third floors—the lower level devoted to the city's culture and life as a railroad town, and the upper level to the science and history of railroading. There is a wonderfully detailed model-train layout on the third level that is set against a Pennsylvania Railroad system map, and the scenery transforms itself as night turns to day. Just down the hall is the testing room, which investigates the ways in which the Pennsy sought to stay competitive—from improving the quality of its track workers' brooms to an investigation into what kind of oranges produced the most juice for its dining cars. Ten dollars buys museum admission and a pass to the **Horseshoe Curve National Historic Landmark,** which is just a few miles west. Pick up directions to the Curve at the museum.

After leaving the railroaders museum, treat your sweet tooth to a quick stop at the **Boyer Candy Company** factory. Boyer produces Mallo Cups: sweet milk chocolate and coconut candies filled with marshmallow crème that come in a bright yellow package. These goodies are an Altoona institution, and the factory store is the place to get them fresh and cheap—in bulk, if you're so inclined, or 45 cents a package.

The Horseshoe Curve landmark is situated just past the Kittanning Reservoir, which provides Altoona's water supply. There's a small gift shop and a scenic viewpoint that can be accessed two ways—by foot up a winding staircase or by funicular tram along a short inclined plane. Though the Pennsylvania Railroad is long gone, the Curve remains active, swinging trains around the mountainside just as it has for more than 150 years. There are three tracks, and trains roll by at least once every 30 minutes, often in opposing directions at the same time. Bring lunch—there are picnic tables and benches trackside.

CURVE BASEBALL

Horseshoe Curve remains an object of local pride in Altoona. The city's minor-league baseball team (the AA affiliate of the Pittsburgh Pirates) is nicknamed the Curve; the team plays at Blair County Ballpark, which is just off PA 36 near the I-99 intersection. Though tickets are inexpensive (under $10), the Curve offers multiple mascots—there's Steamer, Diesel Dog, and personal favorite Al Tuna (get it?), a skinny-legged orange fellow who dances around center field whenever the Curves score a run.

If you've taken the detour to see the Horseshoe Curve, follow Kittanning Point Road back into Altoona and continue traveling crosstown to rejoin PA 36. As you travel north, the scenery changes rapidly from hilly urban to hilly rural. The next significant town is **Patton,** located 18 miles north. It's a quiet place with a few stores, food market, and a public library that opened in 2010. Just before Patton, though, you'll see signs for **Prince Gallitzin State Park.** For a fun diversion to this wonderful state park, make the extremely sharp right turn (almost a complete 180 degrees) and follow the road for 3 miles. You'll spot the recommendable Pirate's Cove Pub and Grill along the way.

The gateway to Prince Gallitzin, which was named for a Russian émigré who served southwest Pennsylvania as a Catholic priest, is a scenic overlook

Prince Gallitzin State Park

of horseshoe-shaped Glendale Lake and is marked by a gazebo. Continue past the skeet club and the environmentally conscious park office (note the solar roof panels and small-scale wind turbine) and explore the park a little. There are lots of recreational opportunities here, including biking, hiking, swimming, and fishing for crappie. In addition to a popular four-hundred-site campground, Prince Gallitzin boasts 10 welcoming cabins near the marina. A couple cabins are lakeside. All in all, this is a well-used, but exceptionally maintained, state park. Prince Gallitzin is also notable for its game lands and bird-watching.

Back on PA 36, stop by the **Seldom Seen Valley Mine,** where underground tours are led by former bituminous-coal miners. Farther down the road, cross the West Branch of the Susquehanna and arrive at the first stop sign for miles in **Mahaffey.** The route here quickly spans three counties, from Clearfield through the northeast corner of Indiana County and into sparsely populated Jefferson County. Aside from a small but significant Amish population (keep your eyes open for Amish baked goods advertised roadside), Jefferson is known mainly for its largest town and the furry little marmot that calls it home. Ten miles past the county line on PA 36 is **Punxsutawney,** which attracts tens of thousands of visitors every year for Groundhog Day festivities in the rolling hills at Gobbler's Knob. As anyone who's seen the hit Bill Murray film knows, each February 2, Punxsutawney Phil is summoned from his tree stump to predict the weather. If Phil sees his shadow, he'll run back inside, signifying six more weeks of winter. If he stays outside, then spring is upon us. In reality, winter always extends six weeks past February 2. Also, life goes on whether or not one is able to woo Andie MacDowell.

Groundhog Day has its roots in groundhog hunting—a popular autumn pastime for the German farmers who inhabited Punxsutawney in the late 19th century. The full story is actually somewhat complex and is derived partly from Pennsylvania groundhog hunting and partly from the Candlemas Day celebrations that descend from the European Catholic tradition. How the old customs were transformed into such a bizarrely intriguing American holiday is an interesting case study for the historically inclined. You can read all about it at **Gobbler's Knob,** where the annual ceremony takes place. There's also a small sculpture exhibit at the Knob, which is two minutes from downtown (traveling north on PA 36, make a left on Woodland Avenue). On Groundhog Day the space is packed from the early morning hours with international media on hand to doc-

Among the many fiberglass Phils in Punxsutawney

ument Phil's prediction. The local Groundhog Club's "Inner Circle" members dress in silk top hats and bow ties to celebrate the occasion as visitors compete for space in the town's few hotels.

The other 364 days a year, Punxsutawney remains a hotbed of groundhog-related kitsch, with flashy human-sized fiberglass groundhogs on display throughout (Punxsutawney Phil with a mailbag at the post office, Phil in a bellhop outfit by the historic Pantall Hotel, etc.) and a tiny Groundhog Zoo in centrally located Barclay Square, where you can see Punxsutawney Phil year-round. Punxsutawney has understandably gone to great lengths to capitalize on its claim to fame, declaring itself Weather Capital of the World. This theme is brought to life at the **Punxsutawney Weather Discovery Center,** a small children's museum housed downtown in a converted post office. There's a do-it-yourself Van de Graaf generator, weather tracking equipment, and other interactive exhibits. For adults the most interesting feature is the building itself—a high-ceilinged Classical Revival–style structure with small charms like the hidden passageways used by supervisors to nab thieving postal workers.

Before groundhog fever found Punxsutawney, she was much like her surrounding western Pennsylvania farming and coal towns. The unique name is an Algonquian term ("town of the sand flies"), but the local Lenape were displaced in the early 19th century. The history that followed revolved mostly around bituminous coal deposits and the town's location on the Mahoning Creek. The **Punxsutawney Historical Society,** located in the Victorian-style Bennis House on PA 36, details the many things once produced around the borough's outskirts, from glass to bricks. With an aging population and a groundhog-based tourist economy limited to a few days a year, Punxsutawney relies increasingly on local assets like a branch of Indiana University of Pennsylvania and its proximity to natural wonders like the Allegheny National Forest. Residents are extraordinarily friendly; happy to talk about the town's past, present, and future; and well versed in groundhog lore.

From Punxsutawney, continue north on 36 and keep your eyes open for a couple roadside curiosities that dot the next 25 miles. One attraction is **Coolspring,** where you can visit the **Coolspring Power Museum,** an authoritative tribute to the internal combustion engine. There are more than 250 examples on display. The museum is only open a couple dozen days a year, so call in advance. The sprawling grounds also play host to an annual summer expo and flea market. The route then passes through **Stanton,** where there isn't much to see, but there's good, inexpensive food at Grandma's Kitchen.

The region's largest town is **Brookville,** the Jefferson County seat. Main Street is a short detour from PA 36, as Brookville's high elevation keeps it at arm's length from nearby I-80. A major lumber town during the industry's heyday, Brookville sports an impressive architectural stock, including the redbrick, Italianate-style courthouse topped by a bell tower. The **Jefferson County Historical Society** on Main Street illuminates the area's agrarian and lumber heritage. Continuing north on PA 36, travel under I-80 and past the usual fast-food chains, which are well represented in the area near the interstate's Brookville exit. Amid all this is **Plylers Restaurant,** which serves an inexpensive buffet. The starters and entrées are unspectacular, but you can't beat the homemade pies for dessert.

The next 10 miles north from Brookville are mostly uneventful. Just past the small town of **Sigel,** things get interesting—you'll begin to see campgrounds, stables, souvenir shops, and eventually motels, water slides, miniature golf courses, and the **Double Diamond Deer Ranch,** where you can observe more than two dozen white-tailed deer up close as well as various stuffed creatures in the adjacent Buck Barn. In the main building, the meticulous owners display the antlers from each animal that ever lived at Double Diamond (completely painless—deer naturally shed their antlers once a year).

This is all a lead-up to **Cook Forest State Park,** a northwest Pennsylvania gem and a popular getaway for families and nature lovers. What makes Cook such a treasure are its trees—some reaching 200 feet and higher. Cook Forest offers a rare chance to see old-growth white pine and hemlock, some of which dates back to the colonial settlement of Pennsylvania. The forest's existence is owed to Anthony Cook, grandson of a lumber industry scion, who lived in the area and vowed to preserve the local strand of virgin timber before Pennsylvania's northern tier was completely despoiled. Cook Forest is a marvelous place to escape. The air is exceptionally crisp, and the tall, thick trees provide great shade, meaning bearable hiking conditions even in the dead of August.

Orient yourself at the park office, which is right on PA 36. The road splits just past this building. You'll probably want to explore the Forest Road prong of this fork to visit the Forest Cathedral, where the virgin white

Cook Forest State Park

pine trees cast their long shadows. There are eight short hiking trails that meander through the Cathedral (longer trails cover the rest of the 8,500-acre park). Most visitors choose the Longfellow Trail, a moderately difficult hike that inclines sharply at first and then levels out. But all Forest Cathedral trails are a fine way to see the pines. Other old-growth trees, including oak and black cherry varieties, can be found elsewhere in the park. Roughly a quarter of the Cook's acreage supports old-growth timber.

At the base of Longfellow Trail is the Log Cabin Inn, an environmental learning center. Peek in and examine the cross section of a three-hundred-year-old tree as well as birds and mammals native to the forest. When you're done with the Forest Cathedral area, head up Tower Road to Seneca Point, a jaw-dropping scenic overlook. It's 1.5 miles off the main road, mostly straight up, which is why the views go right above the treetops. For those who want to go even higher, climb the 80-foot Cook Forest Fire Tower, which was originally designed to scope out forest blazes.

Recreational opportunities abound in Cook Forest, both natural and man-made. The Clarion River makes for a smooth, relaxing canoe ride, and a rental concession is located right near the park office. There's also go-cart racing, minigolf, and a couple pint-sized water parks in the immediate area. The north end of the Cathedral area is a hub for campgrounds and equestrian activity, as well as the **Trail's End** restaurant for casual fare. Nearby, the **Sawmill Craft Center and Theater** offers arts and crafts classes and summer performances. Nearby, the posh **Gateway Lodge** is Clarion County's main choice for a romantic dinner or overnight stay.

IN THE AREA

Accommodations
The market could probably support more and better hotels in the Altoona area, where rack rates exceed what's found elsewhere in central and western Pennsylvania.

Gateway Lodge, 14870 PA 36, Cooksburg. Call 814-744-8017. Tucked discreetly into the Cooksburg woods. Grounds are beautifully landscaped, and the on-site restaurant is held in high esteem. Rooms, suites, and cabins accommodating up to six guests are available. Web site: www.gateway lodge.com.

Attractions and Recreation

Boyer Candy Company, 821 17th Street, Altoona. Call 814-944-9401. Web site: www.boyerscandies.com.

Cook Forest State Park, 113 River Road, Cooksburg. Call 814-744-8407. Web site: www.dcnr.state.pa.us/stateparks/parks/cookforest.aspx.

Coolspring Power Museum, 179 Coolspring Road, Coolspring. Call 814-849-6883. Call ahead for hours. Web site: www.coolspringpower museum.org.

Double Diamond Deer Ranch, 12211 PA 36, Clarington. Call 814-752-6334. Web site: www.doublediamonddeerranch.com.

Horseshoe Curve National Historic Landmark. Call 814-946-0834. Web site: www.railroadcity.com.

Jefferson County Historical Society, 172 E. Main Street, Brookville. Call 814-849-0077. Web site: www.jchonline.org.

Mishler Theatre, 1212 12th Avenue, Altoona. Call 814-949-2787. Web site: www.mishlertheatre.org.

Prince Gallitzin State Park, 966 Marina Road, Patton. Call 814-674-1000. Web site: www.dcnr.state.pa.us/stateparks/parks/princegallitzin .aspx.

Punxsutawney Historical Society, 401 W. Mahoning Street, Punxsutawney. Call 814-938-2555.

Punxsutawney Weather Discovery Center, 201 N. Findley Street, Punxsutawney. Call 814-938-1000. Open Mon.–Tues. and Thurs.–Sat., year-round. Web site: www.weatherdiscovery.org.

Railroaders Memorial Museum, 1300 Ninth Avenue, Altoona. Call 814-946-0834. Open daily, May–Oct.; Fri.–Sun., Nov.–Dec. Web site: www.railroadcity.com.

Sawmill Craft Center and Theater, 140–170 Theatre Lane, Cooksburg. Call 814-927-6655. Web site: www.sawmill.org.

Seldom Seen Valley Mine, Patton. Call 814-247-6305. Web site: www.seldomseenmine.com.

Dining and Nightlife

Plylers Restaurant, 234 Allegheny Boulevard, Brookville. Call 814-849-7357. Recommendable buffet fare, excellent desserts.

Trail's End, 2738 Forest Road, Cooksburg. Call 814-927-8400. Way out there in the Cook Forest hills, this friendly country restaurant is filling and affordable. Open for lunch and dinner. Web site: http://trailsend.cook forest.com.

Other Contacts

Allegheny Mountains Convention and Visitors Bureau, 1 Convention Center Drive, Altoona. Call 800-842-5866. Web site: www.allegheny mountains.com.

Sun sets on the placid Juniata River.

CHAPTER

14

Chasing
the Juniata

Estimated length: 40 miles
Estimated time: ½ day

Getting there: Beginning in Huntingdon, take US 22 east. Just before
Mount Union, switch to PA 522 south, then PA 103 north. Continue on 103
through to Lewistown.

Highlights: This is a leisurely trip along the Juniata River, once a well-
traveled industrial waterway and now among the best fishing rivers in
Pennsylvania. This route connects two county seats—Huntingdon and
Lewistown—passing the Swigart Auto Museum and miles of farmland
along the way.

Pennsylvania's network of rivers and streams is a synthesis of utility and
natural beauty. Major commercial waterways like the Delaware and the
Susquehanna helped power the state's early industrial awakening. Pittsburgh sits at the convergence of the Allegheny and Monongahela rivers into
the Ohio; these rivers made the steel boom possible, opening Pennsylvania to the Great Lakes and the Midwestern manufacturing states. Of course,
long before industrialization, these waterways were a life source for Native
American tribes. The years that followed marked a terrible decline in water
quality as industrialization took a heavy toll on river life. Cleanup efforts in

recent decades have helped reverse the trend, though Pennsylvania still has a ways to go when it comes to the state's most polluted commercial waterways.

On top of its vast rivers and narrow clear-water streams, Pennsylvania also boasts a fair number of intermediate-sized waterways that served a commercial purpose but managed to avoid the near-irremediable exploitation suffered by rivers like the Monongahela. One such example is the Juniata, a 90-mile river that has grown cleaner and more recreationally friendly as the factories that once dumped chemicals into her northwestern branches fade gradually into history. A tributary of the Susquehanna, the Juniata meanders by mountains as it cuts a broad and steady eastward path through the heart of the state. The pleasures of the Juniata stem from its relative isolation, stamped into a narrow valley with population centers few and far between. Its slow pace suggests the passive approach, which is essential to enjoying the river. As Tim Palmer writes in *Rivers of Pennsylvania,* "While the Juniata offers many interesting features, one needs to be either fishing or lazy for full appreciation."

Shallow, slow, and scenic, the Juniata River is rightly considered one of the most beautiful rivers in Pennsylvania. Once used for transportation as both part of the state's Main Line Canal and a backdrop for a Pennsylvania Railroad line, the river now attracts nature enthusiasts for canoeing, camping, bird-watching, and fishing. The ongoing cleanup efforts have been an especially great benefit to sportsmen throughout the region. The river supports an unusually abundant and diverse variety of fish life, including smallmouth bass (its most popular inhabitant), walleye, catfish, carp, and muskellunge. The Juniata is a top-notch fishing destination and attracts anglers from miles around. Some fish from small boats, while others can be found waist deep in the shallow water.

This drive tracks the Upper Juniata, first along relatively populated US 22, and then along the twists and undulations of PA 103, which is as pure a Pennsylvania back road as exists anywhere in the state. While there isn't much in the way of towns or attractions along the way (with the exception of the beginning and end of the drive), there are several opportunities to pull over and take a dip, cast a line, launch a canoe, or just stop to lounge and forget the troubles of the world.

The river takes its name from a Native American word meaning "standing stone." According to legend, local tribes carved their history onto a rock

Juniata College, an economic engine of Huntingdon

almost 15 feet tall, located where the town of **Huntingdon** is now, at the drive's westernmost point. The stone served as a sacred object and a meeting site for the tribes, who held councils here. Huntingdon is also basically where the Juniata forms; the Little Juniata and Frankstown branches meet just northwest of the town and are joined near Huntingdon's eastern edge by the Raystown Branch. This last branch connects the Juniata to hugely popular **Raystown Lake,** which is set against **Trough Creek State Park** (look for directional signs and sport-utility vehicles hauling expensive watercraft near Huntingdon). Like the Juniata itself, the lake is a major fishing destination, and the park boasts fine camping facilities.

Huntingdon remains an important location. As the Huntingdon County seat, the town has the requisite Second Empire–style courthouse and abundance of law firms, but it also counts a number of antiques shops and cafés along its main streets, as well as a nice stretch of park space along the riverbank. Its periphery is dotted with motels and inns, including the recommendable **Huntingdon Motor Inn** and the luxurious **Inn at Solvang.** The area is also home to Juniata College and the **Juniata College Museum of Art,** which houses works of American painters and regional historical photographs, among its many other collections. Huntingdon's vibrant cultural life was a factor in the Coolest Small Town in Pennsylvania designation it earned in a 2009 *Budget Travel* magazine poll.

Herbie the Love Bug at the Swigart Automobile Museum

A few miles east of the Huntingdon business district is **Lincoln Caverns,** home to its namesake cave and the smaller Whispering Rocks Cave, where late caverns owner Myron Dunleavy once delivered Easter sermons. Both are loaded with stalagmite and stalactite formations, and the cave walls have a distinctive orange color, owed to the iron-rich stone that shapes the cave walls. Water drips continuously from the cave ceilings, and the larger cave drops to 120 feet, making for some breathtaking formations. Aboveground is the gift shop with a small snack bar, and an opportunity to pan for gems.

Traveling east along US 22 from Huntingdon, pass **Top's Diner** (one of several quality diners in the Huntingdon area, including **Miller's Diner** east of downtown) and locate the **Swigart Automobile Museum.** Huntingdon native William E. Swigart and his son made their fortune in the insurance business and assembled an extraordinary collection of cars that date back to the earliest days of the automobile production. Three dozen are on display at this nicely executed museum (opened in 1957), though the collection is actually more than four times that size. Start with the 1903 Oldsmobile curved-dash roundabout used by the U.S. Postal Service, and check out the rare 1947 Tucker Prototype, the electric Studebaker, and a beautifully displayed Duesenberg. The museum is also home to license plates from every state and several foreign countries, as well as an original Herbie the Love Bug used in the shooting of the famous Herbie movies (the museum holds title to three of the 20 Herbies in existence).

Twelve miles from Huntingdon, take the turn onto PA 522 south near **Mt. Union,** a small lumber and factory town. It's only a short distance from here to the railroad tracks that mark the sharp left turn onto PA 103 north. PA 103 weaves around the Juniata for the next 28 miles. The 45 mph speed limit is plenty along this stretch, as the many sudden turns and changes in elevation along the base of the Appalachians make this thin two-lane road a lot of fun.

Headed north, the route hugs the edge of the river under an ample canopy of trees. The shaded riverside road is refreshingly cool even in the dog days of summer. Private hunting and fishing clubs are not uncommon along PA 103, a testament to the river's appeal as a choice fishing destination. Boat access areas provide an easy entry into the water, and the Juniata's shallow depth and rocky bottom make for excellent wading. Cornfields and other farmland span the nonriver side of the road, offering impressive vistas from the edges of the rolling hills. Small churches and occasional signs advertising firewood and fresh eggs fill out the scene.

PA 103 continues (largely unmarked, but it's easy to stay on track) through the very small village of **Ryde,** identified exclusively by a small roadside sign. Railroad tracks reemerge around here. There's also the blink-and-you-miss-it small town of **Mattawana** and deeper into the heart of the sparsely populated agricultural region. You can cross the Juniata here to visit **McVeytown** for food and supplies, or continue along 103 past the diverse variety of residences tucked between the trees by the riverbanks. It's a somewhat chaotic assortment. Local professor and fishing enthusiast Dennis P. McIlnay describes the scene well in *Juniata, River of Sorrows:* "The Juniata from McVeytown to Lewistown is lined with every conceivable kind of dwelling, from the primitive to the executive: lean-to's, tents, canopies, huts, storage barns, converted vans and school buses, trailers cottages, and homes.... The more humble the dwellings on the Juniata, the more likely they share another feature: a smoky campfire. *Pennsylachia.*"

Roughly 8 miles from Mattawanna is **Granville,** where you'll notice signs for Malta Park, a lovely community facility with a small stream, volleyball court, and picnic tables. Rolling cornfields, distant mountains, and the odd produce stand provide the backdrop for the remainder of the drive into **Lewistown,** where the route ends. Angelo's Hollow Inn restaurant and a block of row homes mark the gateway to this nine-thousand-person settlement.

Look for Hartley's brand potato chips throughout the region; this kettle-cooked snack has been made in Lewistown since 1935.

Once a bustling hub of cargo transport, Lewistown struggled after the decline of the canal system. The adjustment process has been difficult; a terrible 1972 flood stemming from Hurricane Agnes and subsequent closure of the once dominant American Viscose Company plant (manufacturer of polyester and rayon, and the town's economic driver) dealt a second blow. Today Lewistown is undergoing several rebuilding efforts, including restoration of the beautiful Embassy Theatre, a 1920s picture-palace theater once called the Radio City Music Hall of Central Pennsylvania and a 1998 addition to the National Register of Historic Places. There are several other interesting buildings, including the former Mifflin County Courthouse at the town center. Now home to the Mifflin County His-

Lewistown's Embassy Theatre, a key restoration project

torical Society, the building's grand Ionic columns stand across from a distinctive Civil War memorial. The town could use more amenities, though good, inexpensive food is easy to come by. Fill up at the **Trolley Car Café,** just off the main square.

IN THE AREA

Accommodations

Huntingdon Motor Inn, 6920 Motor Inn Drive, Huntingdon. Call 814-643-1133. A no-frills property, it's a clean, well-maintained motel at half the cost of the nearby Comfort Inn.

The Inn at Solvang, 10611 Standing Stone Road, Huntingdon. Call 814-643-3035. Set back from the street for extra seclusion, this palatial Colonial-style bed & breakfast is just a few miles outside downtown Huntingdon. Web site: www.solvanginn.weebly.com.

Attractions and Recreation

Juniata College Museum of Art, 1700 Moore Street, Huntingdon. Call 814-641-3000. Web site: www.services.juniata.edu/museum.

Lincoln Caverns, 7703 William Penn Highway, Huntingdon. Call 814-643-0268. Open daily, Mar.–Dec., also Jan. and Feb. with advance reservations. Web site: www.lincolncaverns.com.

Swigart Automobile Museum, 12031 William Penn Highway, Huntingdon. Call 814-643-0885. Open daily, May–Oct. Web site: www.swigart museum.com.

Trough Creek State Park, 16362 Little Valley Road, James Creek. Call 814-658-3847. Web site: www.dcnr.state.pa.us/stateparks/parks/trough creek.aspx.

Dining and Nightlife

Miller's Diner, 11740 William Penn Highway, Huntingdon. Call 814-643-3418. Just east of Top's on US 22, Miller's features fresh baked desserts and a weekend breakfast buffet.

Top's Diner, 12165 William Penn Highway, Huntingdon. Call 814-643-4169. Local favorite Top's is the cream of the crop and bottles its home-made sauces to take home.

Trolley Car Café, 15 E. Market Street, Lewistown. Call 717-248-9085. A small diner-style restaurant.

Other Contacts

Huntingdon County Visitors Bureau, 6993 Seven Point Road, Suite 2, Hesston. Call 814-658-0060. Web site: www.raystown.org.

General Buford at the western entrance to Gettysburg National Military Park

CHAPTER

15

A House Divided

Estimated length: 60 miles
Estimated time: 1–2 days

Getting there: Take US 30 from Chambersburg to Gettysburg, then PA 116 past Hanover. PA 116 rejoins US 30. Follow this, and then switch to PA 462 east into York.

Highlights: Primarily a taste of the state's Civil War history, this drive begins in Chambersburg (home base for John Brown prior to his raid on Harpers Ferry) and runs through the storied fields of Gettysburg. It also includes the snack food hot spot of Hanover, where Utz and Snyder's brands are headquartered, and the architectural diversity of York, established in 1741.

In 2001, conservative pundit David Brooks wrote an influential essay for *The Atlantic Monthly,* juxtaposing social trends in Pennsylvania's Franklin County against those of suburban Maryland's Montgomery County. His piece, "One Nation, Slightly Divisible," was the basis for the Red State/Blue State dichotomy that has penetrated popular discourse and is used to frame much of today's politics. Brooks asserted that, broadly drawn, there are two cultural models for understanding America—densely populated, politi-

cally liberal "blue" regions mostly on the coasts, and more rural, conservative "red" areas spread throughout Middle America.

I think about Brooks's piece whenever I visit "red" Franklin County, a
place where he claims to have difficulty spending $20 on a restaurant meal.
Brooks's generalizations paper over some important and interesting
nuances (in a follow-up debunking, a *Philadelphia* magazine reporter spent
$50 on a gourmet prix-fixe dinner at Franklin County's posh Mercersburg
Inn). But at the end of his essay, which was completed shortly after the September 11 attacks, Brooks notes that American flags could be found flying
all over both Franklin and Montgomery counties. Seeing this, he concludes
that maybe we aren't so divided after all.

It's an important point. Because whatever cultural divisions exist in
America today, south-central Pennsylvania is well acquainted with the genuine article. The Civil War comes alive here—most famously the Battle of
Gettysburg in Adams County, but also much of what led up to the crucial
battle and the desperation that followed. The southern Pennsylvania border is just slightly north of the Potomac River, which made it a strategical-
ly important gateway for both the Union and the Confederacy.
Pennsylvania was also a free state bordering a slave state (Maryland) and
became a safe haven for many runaway slaves. A strong abolitionist streak
ran through the Quaker and German communities that inhabited much
of the region. Brooks may be right when he says that coastal elites buy
expensive espresso machines and folks in the heartland do not. But
nobody's going to war over that. This drive explores an era when the big
divisions tore the country apart.

The route begins in **Chambersburg,** an 18,000-person borough that
boasts some remarkable abolitionist history. In 1859 John Brown arrived in
Chambersburg (wearing a bushy beard and presenting himself as "Isaac
Smith") and checked into a small boardinghouse on King Street to plan
his raid on the armory at Harpers Ferry, West Virginia. Posing as a developer of iron mines, he quietly recruited free blacks and abolitionist whites
to the cause. In August of that year he met secretly with Frederick Douglass at a Chambersburg quarry and attempted to secure the abolitionist
leader's support. Douglass declined, calling the plan "sheer madness," but
Brown went ahead with it anyway. The plan was to instigate a slave uprising
using weaponry seized from the armory, but his undermanned brigade was
easily captured. He was hanged on December 2, 1859. It has been argued
that John Brown essentially started the Civil War. The raid on Harpers

Ferry forced the slavery issue to the fore, along with the formation of the abolitionist Republican Party a few years prior.

Regardless, the Confederacy took its revenge on Chambersburg in the summer of 1864. At this late point in the war, the Rebel army was down but not out and decided to make a dramatic statement at Chambersburg. A raid was followed by a demand of $500,000 ransom to preserve the town. The money was not raised, and so the Confederate soldiers torched Chambersburg top to bottom. Fortunately, a handful of historic buildings survived.

The **Franklin County Historical Society**—located in the former county jailhouse—displays artifacts dating back to the burning. You'll find the silverware that one local woman buried amid the chaos and returned 50

The John Brown House in Chambersburg

years later to retrieve. There's other Americana on display here, including a flax spinner and a variety of cookware. If you have roots in the area, check out the extensive research library and see if they have anything on your ancestors. On the ground floor, the historical society has re-created the former Chambersburg apothecary.

The building itself is interesting. A modest Georgian structure built in 1818, it was used continuously as the Franklin County jail through 1970. One cell still contains the scribbling of a former convict, who got 60 days for "damned foolishness" according to his wall writings. He also took the liberty of recording his daily menu for posterity. In the yard are the gallows, which were recently restored but last used in 1912.

I like Chambersburg and recommend exploring it if time allows. The Main Street business strip, essentially between Washington and King streets, includes a good secondhand bookstore; the **Molly Pitcher Waffle Shop,** which serves filling breakfasts and lunches; and some very solid Mexican restaurants (the borough has a sizable Hispanic community). After Chambersburg, proceed east along US 30, also known as the Lincoln Highway.

No book on road travel through Pennsylvania would be complete without a stretch of the Lincoln Highway. Begun in 1912 when unpaved country back roads were the standard for motoring and finished 15 years later in 1927, US Route 30 was the nation's first transcontinental highway, spanning across 12 states en route from Times Square to Lincoln Park in San Francisco. The Lincoln Highway (so named to encourage patriots to support the hefty $10 million project) is arguably America's real Main Street, an unsung and lovely route that recalls a time before six-lane expressways.

Downtown Chambersburg has charm, but it's encircled by chain restaurants and gas stations. That makes the first few miles driving east on US 30 less than scenic. Be patient though—soon enough you'll hit **Caledonia State Park,** a 1,100-acre facility easily accessible off US 30. A main entrance is marked by a small white building capped with a bell tower. This is the Thaddeus Stevens Blacksmith Shop, a rebuilt historic site representing the workshop owned by Stevens—a committed abolitionist and congressman who helped author the 14th amendment to the U.S. Constitution. Stevens also owned the nearby iron furnace, which was destroyed one week before the Battle of Gettysburg by Confederate troops but was re-created in the 1920s. The workshop and the furnace are part of the Thaddeus Stevens Historic Trail, a fun, simple little hike around a piece of Caledonia that merges educational elements with hillside scenery. The trail follows a low stream and then runs along a modest elevation. There are 10 miles of hiking trails in total at the park, including a portion of the Appalachian Trail. In season, rangers and naturalists organize interpretive programming at the park amphitheater, host bird-watching tours, and oversee a terrific campground that rises into the Blue Ridge Mountains. Caledonia is a treasure. Its clever design somehow fashions intimacy and isolation without sacrificing accessibility. It is connected to **Michaux State Forest,** which extends north into Cumberland County.

Past the forest on the opposite side of US 30 is a fun little store. Mister Ed's Elephant Museum displays more than 10,000 of the owner's elephants and doubles as a candy shop. You'll find all kinds of sweet treats, but skip the packaged brand-name candy you can get anywhere and pick up some homemade fudge or freshly roasted peanuts instead. Also, be warned that if you hold off a few minutes, there are more healthful treats to come. South-central Pennsylvania features some of the state's most fertile soil, and a string of orchards extends along both sides of US 30. Sweet cherries, blueberries, peaches, raspberries, strawberries, and plums are all readily available and delicious during the summer months at roadside farm stands. In the early summer, signs advertising CHAMBERSBURG PEACHES can be found throughout the state.

As good as south-central Pennsylvania's fruits and vegetables are, few visit the region just for the produce. The main draw is just up the road, where a bronze statue of Gen. John Buford standing tall and proud signals the gateway to Gettysburg National Military Park. Buford, as the Union general charged with tracking the Confederate Army's northward movements along the Blue Ridge Mountains, was in a sense responsible for the precise location of the battle. But an attack on central Pennsylvania was essentially a foregone conclusion—a calculated risk by Confederate general Robert E. Lee, who saw the summer of 1863 as his best opportunity for an advance on Union soil.

A surprisingly punishing Confederate victory at Chancellorsville in May 1863 had created a unique opportunity. Union troops were on their heels, and the North's failure to end the war quickly was eroding public support. On the other hand, Lee understood that the war's fundamentals disadvantaged his side. With a larger army and a much stronger manufacturing base, the Union had the capacity to fight a lengthy war so long as political support for the effort held. Lee planned to pursue aggressively, win a major battle in the North, and convince European powers like England and France to recognize the Confederacy as an independent country. New-found political legitimacy combined with another strong showing on the battlefield would convince Lincoln to sue for peace and end the thing before the South's long-run disadvantages doomed the Rebels.

That, at least, was the plan. Where exactly the battle would be fought was a secondary concern, so Lee moved the Rebel army north along the Blue Ridge Mountains, waiting for an opportunity. The Union army—specifically General Buford, at the orders of Army of the Potomac general George Meade—forced Lee's hand in the rolling fields outside **Gettysburg.** Over three days in July 1863, the two sides fought the bloodiest, deadliest, and most consequential battle of the Civil War.

The **Gettysburg National Military Park** chronicles the great encounter in exacting detail. Spread over almost 6,000 acres that enclose nearly the entire city of Gettysburg, the park is a triumph of storytelling and design. It has enough material and nuance to satiate the most fanatic Civil War buff but works just as well for a casual cyclist who lacks the slightest interest in the Civil War and just wants a scenic loop. The centerpiece is the $135 million state-of-the-art Museum and Visitor Center, which opened in 2008. It's a good place to start.

But it's not the only place. Just across the street from General Buford on US 30 is a much smaller information center, where (during the summer, at least) you can pick up a park map and talk to a ranger. The map diagrams a 24-mile driving tour, which starts at McPherson Ridge, exactly where US 30 meets the park. It incorporates 16 sites along the way, along with numerous roadside memorials and placards that pay tribute to the many regiments—both Union and Confederate—that participated in the battle. If you go to the Visitor Center and pay a fee ($55 for a single car), a battlefield guide will accompany you on the drive, narrating along the way and stopping at key sites. Without a guide, the driving tour (or AUTO TOUR, as the helpful directional signs call it) is free.

The auto tour pursues a chronological route, following key battle sites and memorials that trace the three-day battle. Without going into too much detail, the first day (July 1, 1863) was a good one for Lee and the Confederates, as they forced the not yet completely assembled Union army south across the city, occupying portions of Gettysburg by nightfall. Day two is counted as a draw, though the Union achieved a major objective by holding Little Round Top—an elevated position on the southeast portion

Taking in the view from Little Round Top

of the battlefield that overlooks the site of Gettysburg's worst skirmishes (known as the Valley of Death). Strategic importance aside, Little Round Top is a favorite stop on the auto tour for its scenic views of the boulder-laden valley, and the beautiful 44th New York Infantry Monument that sits atop the hill. Day three is where the tide fully turned, as Meade's army famously stopped Pickett's Charge, suppressing the Confederates' most aggressive attack on the Army of the Potomac and forcing Lee's retreat to Virginia. Lincoln's dissatisfaction with underappreciated General Meade for electing not to pursue the Rebel Army after Gettysburg is a great story, but a bit beyond the scope of the Gettysburg narrative. The Union victory was decisive enough—if you're acquainted with Civil War history, you'll remember the Battle of Gettysburg as the conflict's turning point. And you'll also remember Lincoln's famed Gettysburg Address, delivered four and a half months after the battle at the site of National Cemetery, where the government had arranged to bury the battle's many fallen soldiers.

Starting with the auto tour and following up with the Museum and Visitor Center is an unconventional approach, but it allows you to fill in the blanks later in the day after you've seen the fields with fresh eyes. And you never know what you'll encounter driving around the battlefield. Costumed interpreters put on periodic demonstrations, and rangers hold informative talks at various locations throughout the park. In the high season there are often special events going on, and the whole three-day battle is reenacted in early July every year.

A ticket to the Museum and Visitor Center ($10.50 for an adult) begins with a video presentation on the battle narrated by Morgan Freeman. Guests are then escorted upstairs to the cyclorama—Paul Philippoteaux's oil on canvas painting portraying Pickett's Charge, wrapped around an entire room. Three hundred and seventy-seven feet long, this incredible piece was created in 1884. The ground-floor museum is similarly well done, a soup-to-nuts look at the Civil War that showcases an expectedly large collection of weaponry, ammunition, battle gear, and related artifacts. One highlight is a display on the uniforms and equipment carried by prototypical Union and Confederate soldiers; the North's industrial advantage becomes readily apparent based on the quantity and quality of his gear. As a Confederate reenactor explained to me once, by the time he reached Gettysburg, two years into the war, a Confederate infantryman might no longer have shoes.

The park is reason enough to visit Gettysburg, but there is a lot to do in town as well. Steeped as it is in history, Gettysburg remains very much alive. The student population at Gettysburg College, which occupies the northwest quadrant of the city, and the year-round tourist trade make for a diverse collection of nonlocals (occupying opposite ends of the age spectrum). First-rate bed & breakfasts like the **Brickhouse Inn** help make the town a year-round draw. And Gettysburg's advantageous location, at the nexus of 10 major crossroads, attracts full-time residents who commute to cities as far off as Baltimore. Architecturally, the city is a mélange of frame houses that survived the battle and brick structures that were built to replace the ones that did not. In the center of town by the main traffic circle is the **David Wills House,** where Abraham Lincoln spent the night before the Gettysburg Address. As the well-told story goes, the day of the cemetery dedication, Harvard president Edward Everett spoke for two hours and Lincoln for two minutes (10 sentences). The president's short speech so perfectly encapsulated the Union's cause that seventh-grade American history students are still required to memorize and deliver it to a classroom of their peers today. I was, at least.

Downtown Gettysburg is packed with other interesting things. Civil War memorabilia stores and art galleries abound, offering opportunities to purchase everything from antique rifles to modernist portraits of Abraham Lincoln. Baltimore Street (US 15) south of the main turning circle is a veritable museum row. I particularly like the **Rupp House History Center** and **Shriver House,** both of which present the battle from the perspective of Gettysburg's civilians. Once the dust had settled and the battle was over, 21,000 wounded soldiers (a third of them Confederates) were spread across the battlefield and the city. Add to that the thousands of unclaimed bodies, dead horses, and a battle-scarred downtown, and one can only begin to contemplate what it was like to live in Gettysburg in the summer of 1863. Buildings were hastily converted into makeshift hospitals. A college professor quipped that the smell was so bad, even the vultures wouldn't come to Gettysburg for weeks after fighting ceased. At the Rupp House you can take a whiff of the peppermint oil that local residents inhaled to cover up the stench.

Because of its association with death, Gettysburg has become something of a hotbed for suspected paranormal activity. In addition to several themed ghost tours and guided ghost hunts, the town is home to the **International Museum of Spiritual Investigations.** This three-room museum displays continually updated photographic evidence of a spiritual presence at various sites throughout the region. There are also displays on the sites deemed "most haunted" in America and around the world.

One site popularly identified as haunted in downtown Gettysburg is the **Jennie Wade House.** The only civilian killed in the Battle of Gettysburg (a stray bullet passed through the home's kitchen door, through her shoulder, and into her heart), Jennie died while preparing bread for Army of the Potomac soldiers. A short house tour notes the home's original fixtures and covers the kitchen, parlor, cellar, and low-ceilinged second floor.

Other notable sites around town include the **Hall of Presidents & First Ladies,** where each chief executive is represented by a life-sized wax model and gets a short voiceover summarizing his term in office. William Howard Taft and Grover Cleveland also get generous tummy tucks. Just down the street is the **Soldiers' National Museum,** which features detailed dioramas of Civil War battle scenes.

Take US 30 through Gettysburg, turning onto PA 116 east just outside the city limits, across Rock Creek and past US 15. It's roughly 15 miles to York County and **Hanover,** the next major town on the drive. A touch worn down but amiable and interesting, Hanover was a disputed territory during part of the colonial period, with its immediate area claimed by both Maryland and Pennsylvania. The dispute engendered disorder and cultivated lawlessness—the area was commonly referred to as Rogue's Roost or Rogue's Rest, attracting tax dodgers and other shady characters. This lasted until the Mason-Dixon Line was established in 1767. Hanover soon became a popular town for German immigrants and thrived on the fertile soil and advantageous central location.

Since its founding, Hanover has been an artisanal manufacturing town, with brick making, tanning, cigar rolling, and other such industries forming its economic core. The manufacturing base has evolved but lives on with the continued success of the snack food industry. Popular independent brands like **Snyder's of Hanover** and **Utz** are based here. Both companies offer factory tours during the week, and their on-site factory outlet stores are a fine place to stock up on the freshest pretzels and potato chips money can buy. The Utz store (just off 116 outside of downtown Hanover) is larger than Snyder's, but both give visitors a crack at free samples and new products you might not find in your local supermarket.

If you aren't stuffed with pretzels, treat yourself to a superb hot dog at the Original Famous Hot Wiener. The diner-style restaurant is located in the small historic district downtown, which is worth a look. Attractive Queen Anne–style buildings and an art deco department store place the town's heyday in the late industrial period through the 1920s. The final segment of the drive runs east from Hanover along 116 and into **Spring Grove,** a two-thousand-resident town that is home to the Glatfelter Paper Company.

The drive terminates in **York,** one of several moderately sized Pennsylvania cities feeling its way through the postindustrial landscape. Significant public resources have been devoted to keeping the assembly lines moving. In addition to the snack foods industry, York is home to **Harley-Davidson's largest motorcycle plant,** which hosts a popular free tour. In fact, the county has dubbed itself Factory Tour Capital of the World for attractions like the Harley plant and the snack food tours at Utz and Snyder's around Hanover. York has also found new life as a home base for commuters employed in greater Baltimore.

The old WPA guide labels York "a town of English birth and German development," like many of her neighbors in the central Pennsylvania farmlands. Its English origin is apparent in the city name as well as its handle (the White Rose City), which is an allusion to the floral symbol on the badge of the House of York in medieval England. It was the state's first village founded west of the Susquehanna River and occupied a well-chosen location in the resource-rich farmlands of the river valley. The year the city was born, the early-Germanic-style Golden Plough Tavern opened on Market Street. The building is still around and easy to pick out: just look for the unusual amalgamation of wooden beams and brick, and the statue of French general Marquis de Lafayette (drink in hand) out front. The tavern is one of dozens of architecturally significant buildings in town.

History buffs love York, not only for the architecture, but for the city's outsized role in several American milestones. The Second Continental Congress fled here during the British occupation of Philadelphia in 1777 and proceeded to write the Articles of Confederation in the city courthouse (not, unfortunately, the courthouse in operation today, though a replica was constructed for the American bicentennial). Around this time York also saw the collapse of the "Conway Cabal"—a fascinating plot by Gen. Horatio Gates and others to steal command of the Revolutionary Army from George Washington. Lafayette's vociferous defense of Washington in front of the Congress at York was a major reason for the scheme's failure, which is why his statue is featured so prominently downtown.

Explore the central city a bit, stopping at notable attractions like the **Police Heritage Museum** and **Fire Museum.** The centrally located **Yorktowne Hotel** remains the toast of Market Street. The **York Expo Center** on the west side hosts the city's annual fair in September and other events throughout the year. And food purveyors gather at the **Central Market,** which is the place to go to pick up fresh meats, cheeses, and produce from local farms. A couple full-service restaurants are located within the market, including the Country Café, which proudly serves pancakes "bigger than your head." And for a quick snack, try Maple Donuts (58 different doughnut varieties) or Bair's fried chicken, the scent of which wafts out onto the Beaver Street entrance, enticing pedestrians to come inside. The market is open Tuesday, Thursday, and Saturday until the early afternoon. Across the street from the market is the **White Rose Bar & Grill,** a modern gas-

Car show at the York Expo Center

tropub popular for Sunday brunch. The extensive menu emphasizes local ingredients, like meat from J. L. Miller Sons—also a Central Market vendor.

IN THE AREA

Accommodations

The Brickhouse Inn, 452 Baltimore Street, Gettysburg. Call 717-338-9337. Among the most popular Gettysburg bed & breakfasts (and there are several), this elegant Victorian property offers 14 rooms spread across two buildings. Web site: www.brickhouseinn.com.

Yorktowne Hotel, 48 E. Market Street, York. Call 717-848-1111. A throwback to a more romantic era for American hotels, this 11-story beauty built in 1925 is among the more prominent buildings of downtown York. It's a full-service hotel with large rooms and a restaurant onsite. Web site: www.yorktowne.com.

Attractions and Recreation

Caledonia State Park, 101 Pine Grove Road, Fayetteville. Call 717-352-2161. Web site: www.dcnr.state.pa.us/stateparks/parks/caledonia.aspx.

Central Market, 34 E. Philadelphia Street, York. Call 717-848-2243. Web site: www.centralmarketyork.com.

David Wills House, 8 Lincoln Square, Gettysburg. Call 866-486-5735. Open daily, May–Aug.; Wed.–Mon., Sept.–Nov. and Mar.–Apr.; and Thurs.–Mon., Dec.–Feb. Web site: www.davidwillshouse.org.

Fire Museum, 757 W. Market Street, York. Call 717-848-5665. Open Sat., Apr.–Nov. or by appointment. Web site: www.yorkheritage.org/vg_fm.asp.

Franklin County Historical Society, 175 E. King Street, Chambersburg. Call 717-264-1667. Web site: http://pafch.tripod.com.

Gettysburg National Military Park, 97 Taneytown Road, Gettysburg. Call 717-334-1124. Open daily, year-round. Web site: Web site: www.nps.gov/gett.

Hall of Presidents & First Ladies, 789 Baltimore Street, Gettysburg. Call 717-334-5717. Web site: www.gettysburgbattlefieldtours.com/hall-of-presidents.php.

Harley-Davidson, 1425 Eden Road, York. Call 717-852-6590. Web site: www.harley-davidson.com/en_US/Content/Pages/Factory_Tours/york.html.

International Museum of Spiritual Investigations, 231 Baltimore Street, Gettysburg. Call 717-398-2026. Web site: www.museumofspirits.com.

Jennie Wade House, 548 Baltimore Street, Gettysburg. Call 717-334-4100. Web site: www.gettysburgbattlefieldtours.com/jennie-wade-house.php.

Michaux State Forest, 10099 Lincoln Way E., Fayetteville. Call 717-352-2211. Web site: www.dcnr.state.pa.us/forestry/stateforests/michaux.aspx.

Police Heritage Museum, 54 W. Market Street, York. Call 717-845-2677. Open Sat., Apr.–Oct. Web site: www.policeheritagemuseum.com.

Rupp House History Center, 451 Baltimore Street, Gettysburg. Call 717-338-1243. Open weekends, May–Aug. Web site: www.friendsof gettysburg.org/therupphistorycenter.html.

Shriver House, 309 Baltimore Street, Gettysburg. Call 717-337-2800. Web site: www.shriverhouse.org.

Snyder's of Hanover, 1250 York Street, Hanover. Call 717-632-4477. Web site: www.snydersofhanover.com.

Soldiers' National Museum, 777 Baltimore Street, Gettysburg. Call 717-334-4890. Web site: www.gettysburgbattlefieldtours.com/soldiers-national-museum.php.

Utz, 900 High Street, Hanover. Call 717-637-6644. Web site: www.utz snacks.com.

York Expo Center, 334 Carlisle Avenue, York. Call 717-848-2596. Web site: www.yorkexpo.com.

Dining and Nightlife

Molly Pitcher Waffle Shop, 109 S. Main Street, Chambersburg. Call 717-261-0067. Well known in the area for chicken and waffles. If you aren't in the mood for a heavy breakfast, they whip up kettle-cooked oats served three ways, alongside the moistest little bran muffins you'll ever have. Open for breakfast and lunch.

White Rose Bar & Grill, 48 N. Beaver Street, York. Call 717-848-5369. Terrific burgers and solid drink specials can be had at this well-located downtown restaurant. It has either a pub feel or a quieter ambience, depending on whether or not a major sporting event is going on. Open for lunch and dinner. Web site: www.whiterosebarandgrill.com.

Other Contacts

Gettysburg Convention & Visitors Bureau, 571 W. Middle Street, Gettysburg. Call 717-334-6274. Web site: www.gettysburg.travel.

Fresh sweet corn—among the many pleasures of Amish country

CHAPTER

16

The Horse and Buggy Trail

Estimated length: 45 miles
Estimated time: 1 day

Getting there: Begin in Intercourse, a hub for Amish tourism. Head west on PA 772, which loops around through Leola, Lititz, Manheim, Mount Joy, and the riverside town of Marietta. From Marietta, find PA 23 east and follow to Lancaster.

Highlights: A tour of the Amish, Mennonite, Brethren, and Moravian villages built into the scenery of enduringly agricultural Lancaster County, the route mostly avoids the tourist hot spots that typify the Pennsylvania Dutch Country tourist region, with the exception of Intercourse.

Backcountry Pennsylvania has a thousand curiosities, but the most distinctive cultural pocket sewn into the landscape is Lancaster County's Amish country. Less than 90 minutes west of Philadelphia in the fertile south-central valley region are America's original Amish settlements: communities devoid of televisions, air-conditioning, and even gas-powered lawnmowers. The old order Amish wear modest clothing, farm their land with horse-drawn tractors, and live in accordance with their principles. While few visitors would trade their cars and computers for life among

the old order Amish, the region's steady tourist traffic betrays a keen interest in this unusually isolated community and its way of life.

Who are the Amish, and where did they come from? Without getting
too deep into the history, the Amish living in Pennsylvania descend from
Anabaptists—a Christian sect organized around adult baptism that
emerged in Switzerland shortly after Martin Luther's criticisms of the
Catholic Church triggered the Protestant Reformation. The Amish were
one of many churches that materialized after divisions within the Anabap-
tist movement broke up the original church. A faction of conservative
Mennonites (a somewhat more flexible sect that shares much of Lancaster
County with the Amish today) broke from their church to form the Amish
community around the time Penn was deeded Pennsylvania. While the
faith's origins date back centuries, the principle of adult baptism remains
central to the canon. Amish children are baptized only after they choose the
church over the modern world. This adolescent process, known as Rum-
springa, can involve separation from the community as Amish youth
explore the world outside the Amish society and must choose to return
(an experience memorably chronicled in the 2002 documentary *Devil's
Playground*).

Pennsylvania's Amish country lies within a larger area inhabited by
the descendants of German and Swiss immigrants who belong to several
Christian sects that made their way across the Atlantic Ocean during the
colony's earliest days. Just beyond the heart of Amish country (and incorporated into this drive) are towns like Lititz, founded by the Moravian
Church, and Ephrata—the brainchild of a single man whose reclusive take
on Christianity lasted just one generation but had a hand in establishing
the town's sizable Brethren community. The Pennsylvania Dutch (a confusing label; *Dutch* is derived from *Deutsche* and relates to the group's German roots) have been living here since William Penn founded
Pennsylvania. Their presence has shaped unique sites and villages throughout Lancaster County, all of which are worth visiting.

Still, most visitors are drawn here by their curiosity of the Amish. The
region has remained the American hub for Amish culture, even as high
birth rates and the dwindling availability of affordable farmland have pro-
voked a move westward. States like Ohio, Indiana, and Missouri all have
significant (and expanding) Amish settlements, but Pennsylvania remains
the first and largest. Approximately one quarter of the American Amish live
in Pennsylvania. The areas around original Amish settlements in the east-

ern portion of Lancaster County have changed somewhat, but the Amish community lives on much as it has since its arrival.

It hardly bears mentioning that the Amish take their faith seriously. They are motivated by a steadfast belief in the natural rewards that flow from hard work, a commitment to family, and an unwavering humility before God. These ideals are central to everyday lives of the Amish and explain their rejection of any technology deemed threatening to the group's value system. Colorful clothing, electricity, radios, and automobiles are among the many proscribed items and conveniences in the Amish community. Lancaster County's Mennonites, who maintain the essential ethos of the old order Amish, are more flexible when it comes to modern technology. You'll see modestly dressed Mennonite families in minivans and Mennonite farmers tilling their fields with gas-powered tractors.

The Amish and the Mennonites came to Pennsylvania for the same reason that minority groups have been flocking here since the colony's founding: a chance to live in peace without abandoning an identity. Despite an unconventional worldview and lifestyle, the Lancaster County Amish have managed to coexist with the neighboring majority for centuries. Debates within the community often involve the minor compromises made to accommodate the modernity that surrounds them. Some Amish businesses, for example, accept credit cards. Others do not. Heavily Amish areas like Lancaster County have also made gestures toward accommodating the old order settlements; one practical consideration to take into account in Amish Country is the ever-present flow of horse-drawn buggies encroaching from the road shoulder into automobile traffic (or perhaps it is the other way around). Do keep an eye out, and bear in mind that the carriages move slowly relative to cars and trucks.

An interest in Amish culture is only one reason to take this drive. Delicious food and gorgeous rolling countryside are two more. Appetizingly high-calorie Pennsylvania Dutch Country treats like fried chicken, mashed potatoes, and buttered noodles are served fresh in markets and restaurants throughout the region. Sweet corn and eggs are sold roadside in the summertime, and pies are baked and sold the day the fruit comes off the branch or vine. Wash it all down with Amish root beer, which has a little bite and cuts through a hazy day like a sharp knife.

And about that gorgeous rolling countryside—it's there because the Amish can be counted on to keep their land. A great deal of rural Pennsylvania acreage, particularly in the state's populous south-central and south-

Farmland in Lancaster County

east region, has been converted into sprawling housing developments and shopping malls. But the big-box retail developer who's depending on the Amish to sell him their farmland will not stay in business for long. Meanwhile, the Amish and Mennonite presence so close to greater Philadelphia has benefitted even those city dwellers who never venture a hour west to see Amish country—as any Philadelphian who has purchased produce from a Lancaster County farmer at downtown's Reading Terminal Market will tell you.

The area has been a popular tourist destination for some time. And Lancaster County's Amish have, by and large, come to terms with the throngs of visitors who vacation here year-round to see them. Some earn money selling their wares—often high-quality furniture and quilts—or produce, jams, and baked goods. Others offer horse-drawn buggy tours. The most authentic way to interact with the Amish is to find a bed & breakfast that maintains a relationship with local Amish families and ask to share a meal with one (the **Carriage Corner** in Intercourse is one such option).

When it comes to Amish country tourism, the strip along PA 340 near the town of Bird-in-Hand is the most heavily trafficked. This is where attractions like the Amish Experience at Plain & Fancy Farm put a neatly packaged gloss on Amish life, offering film presentations, interpretive sites, dining, and bus tours. A luxury hotel (the Amish View Inn & Suites) rounds things out. Attractions like Plain & Fancy Farm are popular with families and school groups.

This tour avoids Bird-in-Hand, but it does begin in nearby **Intercourse,** another Lancaster County village that actively courts the tourist trade. Its improbable name is believed to reference its placement at the junction of two major state roads. The **Amish Mennonite Information Center** is headquartered here and offers educational materials on the local culture and religious traditions. The town itself is packed with gift shops and food purveyors like the Intercourse Canning Company (relishes, salsas, etc.) and the Intercourse Pretzel Factory, where visitors can try their hand at the deceptively nuanced art of pretzel making. Most intriguing are the museums, some related to the Amish and others not. The **People's Place Quilt Museum** does a thorough job conveying the artistry and time involved in producing an Amish quilt. A large gift shop on the lower level distinguishes itself from the town's many craft stores with its varied samplers and faceless Amish dolls (meant to stress the virtues of humility). For something completely different, stop by the **American Military Edged Weaponry Museum,** at the intersection of PA 340 and 772, and check out the impressive variety of pistols, knives, and other military paraphernalia packed into a single large room. Following 772 west out of Intercourse, you'll see the tour buses assemble in **Kitchen Kettle Village,** a shopping and dining plaza with more than three dozen stores and 15 hotel rooms.

PA 772 makes for a wonderful drive. The 34 miles from Intercourse to the road's terminus in western Lancaster County are the best of all worlds: a unique assortment of small towns linked by a simple two-lane road and seemingly infinite country scenery. Corn fields and dairy farms emerge less than a mile from Intercourse, though you'll find a clustering of furniture merchants and crafts stores a little more removed from the town center. Come upon the **Mascot Roller Mills and Ressler Family Home** and stop in for a free tour. The old grain mill still functions, though it stopped grinding flour in 1977. The house next door is a similarly authentic look at rural life in the region, with period antiques and an engaging narrative about the gracious Ressler family, who owned the mill. Picnic across the street by Mill Creek and look for blue heron.

Proceed along 772, and pass over the railroad tracks just outside **Leola.** Shortly after the road crosses the Conestoga River is a terrific diversion. Look for PA 272, which will appear soon after the entrance ramp to the US 222 expressway. Follow 272 north approximately 5 miles to **Ephrata** and watch for signs directing traffic toward the **Ephrata Cloister.** The cloister tells the story of Johann Conrad Beissel and his dyed-in-the-wool followers who lived a zealously simple existence in Ephrata, sleeping on wooden planks and rising every night from midnight to 2 AM—the hour at which Beissel had promised them the Second Coming of Christ. The customs described by the white-robed guides on the hour-long tour of the cloister grounds paint a fascinating portrait of his lost sect. Beissel enforced mandatory celibacy, which taken alongside the harsh, lonely life at the hermitage sealed the faith's ultimate demise. But Ephrata attracted Brethren and Mennonite congregations as well, and the area retains this influence today. Just beyond downtown is the rambling **Green Dragon farmer's market,** a fine place to browse for produce and crafts on Friday (the only day of operation). If you need a little more to meet your shopping fix, continue north on 272 another 9 miles from Ephrata to **Adamstown,** where the streets are lined with antiques shops. Either way, this side trip to should be completed in a half day or less; once you're done, return to 772 and continue west.

Soon enough you'll find yourself in **Lititz,** a personal favorite. This beautifully preserved small town is best known today for its ready supply of fresh chocolate. Adjacent to the former Lititz train station and a nicely landscaped park, the century-old **Wilbur Chocolate Factory** remains operational. Highly popular, especially around the holidays, Wilbur offers an opportunity to see the confectionary process in action and to load up on freshly made treats. Right nearby is **Café Chocolate of Lititz,** which puts the good stuff to creative use, incorporating rich dark chocolate into several inventive main courses and desserts.

Chocolate may be Lititz's most prominent identity, but it's not the town's first. A century and a half prior to Wilbur's arrival, the Moravian Church came to Lititz from Bethlehem to build the kind of self-sufficient

The old Lititz railroad station next door to Wilbur Chocolate

Christian community that had taken hold throughout rural Pennsylvania in the decades following Penn's progressive charter. The Moravians built a church 30 years later, which survived a 1957 fire and stands today. A famously thrifty people whose European roots predate Martin Luther's grievances against the Catholic Church, the Moravians rejected property rights and imposed a highly regimented social structure on its membership. As one example, the town leadership permitted only a single craftsman to practice each trade in Lititz at any given time, which is how a gentleman named Johannes Mueller became the town's only dyer of cloth. You can tour the house where Mueller lived and the adjacent **Lititz Museum** on Main Street to learn more about the village's Moravian founding and the changes that followed. A century after its creation, Lititz and its

Moravian inhabitants were joined by Lutheran and Brethren congregations. The town continued to flourish as an industrial and agricultural center. It was an early site for pretzel making and still produces terrific snacks at the Julius Sturgis Pretzel Bakery (America's first commercial pretzel factory).

But more than anything else, Lititz is worth visiting because it embodies the best of small-town Pennsylvania. Its people are exceptionally welcoming, and their enthusiasm for the town resonates everywhere: its active civic associations, frequent community events, and an exceptional shopping district that is as interesting for visitors as it is useful for residents. The original Germanic and Federal buildings found in the historic district are a testament to the significant efforts made to preserve the town's intimate old-world feel. Lavish, meticulously maintained bed & breakfasts like **Swiss Woods** can be found tucked in the countryside. True, Lititz has benefitted from economic advantages (including Amish country tourist traffic), but there are well-to-do villages in all corners of the state that have failed to apply such attentiveness to their preservation efforts. Many Pennsylvania towns are nice. Lititz is special.

Continuing westward on PA 772, Lititz is followed by the three M's—**Manheim, Mount Joy,** and **Marietta.** They are separated from one another by 5 or 6 miles each, as farmland, churches, and exurban housing developments fill out the landscape (the Amish presence is not as concentrated in western Lancaster County). Manheim is a tidy and orderly borough. Like many regional villages, it was settled by German immigrants in the mid-18th century. Unlike Lititz or Ephrata, however, it lacked an overtly religious raison d'être. A diverse manufacturing base evolved from glassmaking, Manheim's original economic anchor. The annual **Pennsylvania Renaissance Faire** attracts big crowds 5.5 miles north of Manheim at the Mount Hope Estate and Winery every weekend from mid-August to October.

Compared with the surrounding settlements in western Lancaster County, Mount Joy is the most suburban in appearance—the business district, home to some worthwhile antiques shops and crafts stores, is spread out more than those of neighboring towns. Note the Reist Popcorn Company factory as you arrive on 772, another fine contribution to the region's well-deserved reputation for high-quality snack-food production. The route swings left past a stone Lutheran church and opens up a little as it leaves Mount Joy, with speed limits peaking at 55 miles per hour.

The most intriguing western Lancaster town is Marietta, which lies past the end of PA 772 on the banks of the Susquehanna River. The key development in Marietta's history was the completion of the Philadelphia & Columbia Railroad, which terminated just a few miles southeast. The railroad's opening in 1834 completed the Main Line of Public Works, making Marietta a vital transport point linking the Pennsylvania Canal to the railroad. It became a somewhat rowdy town during this period and played a significant role in the development of Pennsylvania's lumber and iron industries. As often happened in such settlements, a white-collar class associated with the blossoming manufacturing economy brought Victorian architecture to Marietta in the latter part of the 19th century. The annual **Marietta Candlelight Tour** is held on the first Sunday in December and is the definitive way to see the expansive historic district, which covers close to half the town.

Marietta was formed from three separate villages in the early 19th century, which contributed to a unique layout. Narrow streets and discontinuous access to the river make it worth walking around and exploring. The other side of the coin is that the slightly counterintuitive design can make it difficult to find your way out. Locate Market Street, and proceed east. The road soon becomes PA 23 south, which is the last segment of this drive. It is 13 miles to **Lancaster** along a fun little stretch spotted with produce sales and comfort-food restaurants. Most of the action is concentrated around the small community of **Silver Spring,** half the way down PA 23.

The first sign of Lancaster is **Wheatland,** the retirement home of President James Buchanan. Many scholars cite Buchanan as the worst president in American history for his ineffectual leadership style and indecisiveness on the slavery question in particular. A compromise candidate of the Democrat party, Buchanan's hands-off approach was ill suited to managing a contentious pre–Civil War America. His lackluster term in office capped an otherwise distinguished career as a lawyer, congressman, senator, and diplomat to Great Britain and Russia. Most of that has been forgotten, though, and Buchanan's place in the history books is dominated by two exclusive claims: first, as America's only bachelor president, and second, as the lone president ever elected from Pennsylvania.

Wheatland is a handsome Federal-style country mansion a couple miles west of downtown Lancaster, and it's well worth visiting if you have an interest in American history or seeing the estate's original Victorian furnishings. Tours are conducted by costumed guides who expound on Buchanan's life and presidency, including the story of his niece Harriet Lane, who became the White House's de facto first lady during his term in office and who accompanied her uncle back to Wheatland post-presidency.

Downtown Lancaster concludes the tour just down the road. The Red Rose City is a fun, spirited little place that maintains remnants of its initial agricultural-oriented economy alongside manufacturing, transportation, university, and service-sector activities that form the bulk of the modern jobs base. Though it has changed over the years, Lancaster has known neither explosive growth nor crippling disinvestment (its population has hovered between 55,000 and 65,000 people for the last 80 years). Queen Street and Prince Street are the main north–south arteries, and King Street runs east–west (like rival city York, Lancaster got its name from monarchical England). A diverse city from its earliest days, Lancaster was home to stops on the Underground Railroad more than a half century prior to the Civil War. Steeples peek out above the redbrick Federal-style row homes in all

Wheatland estate on a snowy December day

directions, and audible chimes mark the hours—Lancaster has more than five dozen churches downtown, representing a wide range of religious traditions. The city was also colonial America's capital for a single day; the Continental Congress met here during the British siege of Philadelphia before resuming their escape to York.

Like York, Lancaster has a bustling Central Market where locals and visitors alike assemble to purchase high-quality foods produced nearby. Dining is a local strong suit generally, and restaurants in Lancaster are more eclectic than one normally finds in south-central Pennsylvania; impressive Ethiopian and Mexican options exist (try La Cocina Mexicana near the Central Market). There is less Pennsylvania Dutch cuisine than expected, but other local entrepreneurs have taken ample advantage of Lancaster's ready access to fresh ingredients. **Carmen & David's Creamery,** a colorful ice cream parlor on Prince Street, dips phenomenal homemade ice cream and offers it served in pretzel cones. Across the street is the **Fulton Theatre,** a national historic landmark and premiere regional venue for plays, musicals, and the Lancaster Symphony Orchestra.

IN THE AREA

Accommodations

Carriage Corner Bed & Breakfast, 3705 E. Newport Road, Intercourse. Call 800-209-3059. Located just outside central Intercourse, this country-style inn boasts five impeccably maintained rooms and knowledgeable innkeepers with deep roots in the area. Web site: www.carriagecorner bandb.com.

Swiss Woods Bed & Breakfast and Inn, 500 Blantz Road, Lititz. Call 717-627-3358. A lush country getaway in the Lititz hills, furnished with Swiss paraphernalia and regionally famous for its superb breakfasts. The large guest rooms are built with soft woods that create a warm, welcoming feel. Web site: www.swisswoods.com.

Attractions and Recreation

American Military Edged Weaponry Museum, 3562 Old Philadelphia Pike, Intercourse. Call 717-768-7185. Open Mon.–Sat., May–Nov.

Ephrata Cloister, 632 W. Main Street, Ephrata. Call 717-733-6600. Open daily, May–Oct.; Tues.–Sun., Mar.–Apr. and Nov.–Dec.; and Wed.–Sat., Jan.–Feb. Web site: www.ephratacloister.org.

Fulton Theatre, 12 N. Prince Street, Lancaster. Call 717-394-3234. Web site: www.fultontheatre.org.

Green Dragon farmer's market, 955 N. State Street, Ephrata. Call 717-738-1117. Web site: www.greendragonmarket.com.

Kitchen Kettle Village, 3529 Old Philadelphia Pike, Intercourse. Call 717-768-8261. Web site: www.kitchenkettle.com.

Lititz Museum, 137–145 E. Main Street, Lititz. Call 717-627-4636. Open Mon.–Sat., May–Oct. Web site: www.lititzhistoricalfoundation.com.

Marietta Candlelight Tour. Call 717-426-4048. Web site: www.marietta restoration.org.

Mascot Roller Mills and Ressler Family Home, 443 W. Newport Road, Ronks. Call 717-656-7616. Open Tues.–Sat., May–Oct. Web site: www.resslermill.com.

Pennsylvania Renaissance Faire, 2775 Lebanon Road, Manheim. Call 717-665-7021. Web site: www.parenfaire.com.

People's Place Quilt Museum, 3510 Old Philadelphia Pike, Intercourse. Call 800-828-8218. Open Mon.–Sat., year-round. Web site: www.ppquilt museum.com.

Wheatland, 230 N. President Avenue, Lancaster. Call 717-392-4633. Open Mon.–Sat., Apr.–Oct.; Fri.–Sat. in Nov. Web site: www.lancaster history.org.

Wilbur Chocolate Factory, 48 N. Broad Street, Lititz. Call 717-626-3249. Web site: www.wilburbuds.com.

Dining and Nightlife

Café Chocolate of Lititz, 40 E. Main Street, Lititz. Call 717-626-0123. They do incredible things with dark chocolate here, working the stuff into all three meals and exceptional desserts. Hot chocolate is naturally superb and an essential complement to any meal. Open for breakfast, lunch, and dinner. Web site: www.chocolatelititz.com.

Carmen & David's Creamery, 25 N. Prince Street, Lancaster. Call 717-393-2015. Web site: www.carmenanddavidscreamery.com.

Other Contacts

Amish Mennonite Information Center, Old Philadelphia Pike, Intercourse. Call 717-768-0807. Web site: www.mennoniteinfoctr.com.

Pennsylvania Dutch Convention & Visitors Bureau, 501 Greenfield Road, Lancaster. Call 717-299-8901 or 800-723-8824. Web site: www.pa dutchcountry.com.

A patriot mural in Kennett Square

CHAPTER

17

Revolutionary Road

Estimated length: 25 miles
Estimated time: ½ day to full day

Getting there: Begin the trip in Kennett Square, the westernmost of the Brandywine Valley towns. Drive north on PA 82 for 8 miles. Switch to PA 842 east, and follow through to downtown West Chester. Take Paoli Pike out of West Chester, continuing east. At US 30, the route hits Paoli. Continue east on 30 briefly and then transfer onto PA 252 north. Follow this through to Valley Forge National Historical Park.

Highlights: This drive takes some liberties with the chronology but mostly tracks the Philadelphia Campaign undertaken by British troops around the Philadelphia countryside in 1777. It includes stops at Paoli Battlefield, where Gen. Anthony Wayne's contingent was famously massacred, and Valley Forge National Historical Park, the site of George Washington's winter encampment after a string of defeats forced the Revolutionary Army into retreat.

Pennsylvania's outsized role in American history spans all eras and activities, from the technological to the political. Imagining an America without railroads is as unfathomable as imagining an America without the Second Continental Congress. The state's military history is similarly pertinent. As the Founding Fathers deliberated in Philadelphia, the American Revolution was being fought in the countryside. The Battle of Trenton—an early success—was formulated on the Pennsylvania side of the Delaware River in what was then known as Taylorsville. It would be the state's most triumphant contribution to the military effort but far from the last.

This final drive through Chester County follows a few extremely bleak months of the American Revolution from the fall of 1777 through the winter of 1778, when the theater of war returned to southeast Pennsylvania. The British Army began the Philadelphia campaign in late August 1777, marching up from Maryland and Delaware into the Pennsylvania countryside to attempt a march on the city (the patriots' capital city during the Revolutionary War). The British Army took Philadelphia barely a month later and occupied it through the spring of 1778, compelling the Continental Congress to flee to York and crippling Washington's already hobbled supply chain. But despite a crushing defeat at Paoli, bookended by tough losses at the Battle of Brandywine and the Battle of Germantown, these months famously demonstrated the Continental Army's resilience. The period culminated with the encampment that winter at Valley Forge; a difficult time for the Continentals, but a period widely cited today as the revolution's turning point. Surviving these darkest hours made the eventual victory possible.

The region as it now stands, incorporating parts of the area known as the Brandywine Valley, is made up of elegant small towns and well-heeled Philadelphia suburbs. Scattered throughout the lush Brandywine scenery are nods to the Revolutionary history that took place here. How long this drive takes will depend largely on one's interest in the military history. Distance wise, this is the shortest drive in the book. That said, the route's end point at Valley Forge National Historical Park can easily occupy an entire day by itself.

Begin in **Kennett Square,** just a couple miles from famous **Longwood Gardens** and home to the majority of America's cultivated mushroom production. Advantageously located amidst the Brandywine Valley fields at the nexus of US 1 and PA 82, Kennett Square is a highly livable community and a well-regarded weekend getaway for Philadelphians. Mushrooms first arrived here by way of a local farmer whose lone spawn (acquired during a trip to England) has boomed into a hugely lucrative industry for the town. Kennett restaurants like the **Half Moon Restaurant and Saloon** and famed **Talula's Table** make a point of incorporating local mushrooms in their meals, and an entire store (the **Mushroom Cap**) offers diverse varieties at excellent prices alongside mushroom-related souvenirs. An annual mushroom festival is held in Kennett Square every Labor Day weekend. As for the gardens, try and visit during a special event like Independence Day, when fireworks and musical accompaniment enhance the beautiful grounds. The Philadelphia Orchestra plays here on occasion as well. Longwood can be toured year-round and is always a treat, located just east of downtown Kennett Square along US 1. Half a dozen quality bed & breakfasts make spending the night in Kennett Square an attractive option; **Bancroft Manor** and the **Stebbins-Swayne House** are a couple good choices.

Kennett Square is also where Gen. William Howe and the redcoats began their march east to Chadds Ford in September of 1777 to attack General Washington and the Revolutionary Army. The Battle of Brandywine, as it came to be known, was an equivocal British success. Major Continental troop losses forced Washington back on his heels, but Howe's decision to allow an easy retreat brought strong criticism from across the Atlantic and from Loyalists in the colonies. Those so inclined can learn more about the battle at **Brandywine Battlefield State Park,** which is a 7-mile side trip east of Kennett Square on US 1 to the Brandywine Valley town of **Chadds Ford.** State budget cuts have forced the park to close for all but special events. There are, however, other notable Revolutionary-era sites around Chadds Ford, such as historic local churches and General Howe's headquarters.

If you are unable to tour the park, take the prearranged route north on PA 82 through greater Kennett Square. Bicyclists are a common sight along the shoulder—the spacious suburban communities of Chester County make for great rides so long as one appreciates the occasional ups and downs. Past the Kennett Square Golf & Country Club and the PA 926 intersection, a turning circle directs PA 82 through **Unionville.** Make the right turn onto PA 842 east here, and watch the scenery turn a little more pastoral. Pick up sweet corn and other local produce at **Northbrook Marketplace,** a converted barn and a terrific resource not only for fruits and vegetables, but also cheeses, baked goods, farm fresh eggs, and scrumptious prepared meals that can be enjoyed at the picnic tables either inside or outside the marketplace.

Follow PA 842 through to **West Chester,** a larger Brandywine town that witnessed no military combat during the revolution, but it stands at the heart of the troop movements and supply sites that shaped the contours of battle in the fall of 1777. Today it's a fine place to stop for food, drink, and a dose of local history at the top-notch **Chester County Historical Society** museum, which showcases the area's estimable tradition of racial tolerance. Prosperous and handsome, West Chester is the county seat and home to West Chester University; the school boasts a large student body that rivals the borough's year-round population in size. A healthy mix of upper middle class professionals and mostly well-behaved students populate the downtown blocks and support the several bars and restaurants, such as **Spence Café.** Neatly constructed redbrick Greek Revival– and Federal-style buildings around the business district make West Chester a model small town—parts of the film *Marley & Me* were shot here in 2008, with downtown West Chester presented as Kalamazoo, Michigan. A seasonal Saturday-morning walking tour explores the local architecture.

You'll enter West Chester at Everhart Park and continue through the business district. In addition to the restaurants, shopping may be of interest here. Unusual crafts and gift stores are scattered around town, as well as high-quality food purveyors like Éclat Chocolate on High Street. High is one of three major streets—Gay Street and Market Street (running parallel to one another) are the other two.

As you leave downtown West Chester, look for a large green traffic sign on the left hand side of the road indicating Paoli Pike. This road connects West Chester to the region's next major Revolutionary War site. As you pass the shopping centers and restaurants along the way, look for turnoff signs to the **American Helicopter Museum** and **QVC Studio Park** (both are accessible via a left on Airport Road). The first of these tracks the history of rotary wing aircraft through exhibit space and actual military helicopters for kids to climb into and imagine flying. And just down the road is the headquarters for the eminent home shopping television station, which broadcasts from greater West Chester 24 hours a day. You can tour the studio daily and might be able to catch a live taping if you call ahead and make a reservation.

Back on Paoli Pike, return to a Revolutionary-era frame of mind: consider Washington's army, defeated at the Battle of the Brandywine, and forced into retreat. The general was, at this point, mostly just desperate to keep Philadelphia safe and ward off British forces that had gained strength relative to that of the Continental Army after Brandywine. Washington camped out in Malvern (just up the road from West Chester along Paoli Pike) and faced a potentially devastating blow five days after the skirmish at

Chadds Ford, when Howe's army planned to strike the Continentals at what came to be known as the Battle of the Clouds. It wasn't much of a battle; inclement weather kept Howe from attacking with full force, and Washington used the turn of luck to retreat farther into the outskirts of Philadelphia (to an area later annexed by the city). From here he fortified his troops and attempted to guard the American capital. He left behind Gen. Anthony Wayne and a single troop division in Malvern. The idea was to fend off Howe as much as possible to slow his march to Philadelphia and allow Washington to defend the city properly.

In years subsequent to his Revolutionary War service, General Wayne has been memorialized and honored throughout Pennsylvania—the Main Line town of Wayne, the county of Wayne in the state's northeast corner, and Waynesburg borough in the southwest are among the many places named for the general (a Pennsylvania native son who grew up in Chester County). But this required a rehabilitation of his character that came only after a court martial following the fall of 1777. Shortly after Washington left Wayne and approximately 1,500 troops camped out in the vicinity of Malvern and Paoli, the Continentals were humiliated by a British contingent. A surprise attack in the late evening of September 20 was perfectly timed to inflict maximal damage on Wayne's division. In what came to be known as the Paoli Massacre more than 250 Continental troops were killed, wounded, or captured while barely any British troops were harmed. Encamped in an open field, susceptible to attack and lacking a logical retreat, the Continentals were killed mostly with bayonets and swords. The violence inflicted on Wayne's division was unusually severe. Because of the brutality, the events at Paoli came to embody exactly what colonists detested about the British. Soldiers and patriots would chant "Remember Paoli" for the remainder of the war effort. Wayne was accused of negligence by rivals within the Continental Army for his performance at Paoli, but he defended himself successfully at a court of inquiry later that fall and remained an asset to Washington for the remainder of the revolution and the years that followed.

The **Paoli Battlefield** has been preserved and is located just off Paoli Pike. Directional signs are clear—look for Sugartown Road, where the Phelps School and the Sugartown Veterinary Hospital are located. Make the left, and then a right shortly thereafter onto Monument Road. This will take you to the battlefield, which has been left much as it was in 1777—an open space surrounded by woods. There is a memorial on-site, a short hiking trail through the woods surrounding the field, and split-rail fences reconstructed to evoke the Revolutionary era.

Were this drive to remain perfectly accurate in a chronological sense, it would proceed next to Germantown. This northwest Philadelphia neighborhood (then an independent village) was the next front in the British campaign to take what was then the American capital. The redcoats captured Philadelphia easily after Paoli. The October 4, 1777, Battle of Germantown—a last-gasp sneak attack by Washington to retake the city—was unsuccessful. Germantown's Cliveden is a great attraction and a must-see for those interested in learning about the battle and seeing the battlefield. But getting to Germantown from Paoli is a 22-mile trip and logistically complicated. Return instead to Paoli Pike and continue east, through downtown **Paoli** (the western terminus of Philadelphia's most famous commuter train line) and very briefly along US 30 east until you come upon the intersection with PA 252 north. Make the left and travel the 7 miles along 252 to **Valley Forge National Historical Park,** hanging right at the US 202 intersection and passing the low-rise hotels and affluent

Split-rail fences at Paoli Battlefield

housing developments that make up the village of **Valley Forge** today.

Valley Forge is where Washington brought the Continental Army to regroup and retrain after the disappointing fall of 1777. The idea was to find an easily defensible (meaning high elevation) encampment several miles from Philadelphia. Valley Forge fit the bill. From here Washington could receive intelligence about British activities within the occupied city while maintaining enough distance to guard against an attack. The winter was harsh, and troops faced shortages in clothing, food, and other supplies. But the time away from battle helped heal and professionalize the army, as Washington brought in foreign officers like Prussian general Baron Friedrich Wilhelm von Steuben to drill the Continentals. The national historic park is a 3,500-acre facility that serves the dual purposes of education and recreation. Revolutionary-era sites, memorials, statues, reconstructed log huts, barns, and historic markers can be found throughout. Popular bike and foot trails loop around most of the outer ring. The Schuylkill River separates the park's southern portion, where most historical attractions are located, from the smaller northern section.

PA 252 ends at its intersection with PA 23 inside the park. Follow 23 east approximately 2 miles from here and begin touring the park at the nicely remodeled visitors center (really a small museum). A video presentation introduces the subject matter and exhibits cover the history, presenting weaponry and tools dating back to Washington's encampment. Pick up a park map and consider purchasing a driving tour CD that provides commentary and reinforces driving directions. Guided trolley tours also leave from here if you want to leave the driving to someone else.

Otherwise, just leave the visitors center and explore the park as little or as much as you like. Look for the ENCAMPMENT TOUR signs found along the roadside, which direct visitors along the preferred route. You'll pass several reconstructed log huts modeled after the shelters built by the Continentals (the originals were built far too quickly to last very long). Good old "Mad" Anthony Wayne gets a statue of his own on the south edge of the park halfway between the National Memorial Arch (built in 1917 prior to Valley Forge's designation as a national historic park) and an attractive covered bridge that crosses Valley Creek. Washington's headquarters beside the Schuylkill are another highlight. The informational panels that accompany most historic areas make it easy to appreciate the park on bicycle or foot. On all but the gloomiest days you are likely to see locals making use of the paved paths.

Knox–Valley Forge Dam Covered Bridge

Visitors are also exceedingly likely to spot the gangs of white-tailed deer that have taken to the park and trod throughout. Overpopulation is a significant problem; the deer have become nonchalant around cars and people, and often venture onto the adjacent state roads. This creates a minor safety hazard and something to be cognizant of while driving in and around the park.

IN THE AREA

Accommodations

Bancroft Manor, 318 Marshall Street, Kennett Square. Call 610-470-4297. One of several fine Victorian inns in Kennett Square, Bancroft features original leaded-glass windows and an attractively furnished parlor room. Web site: www.bancroftmanor.com.

Stebbins-Swayne House, 221 S. Union Street, Kennett Square. Call 610-444-9097. There are three rooms to choose from at this handsome Georgian-style Kennett Square B&B. Fresh produce from the yard is incorporated into the breakfasts when possible. Web site: www.sshbandb.com.

Attractions and Recreation

American Helicopter Museum, 1220 American Boulevard, West Chester. Call 610-436-9600. Open Wed.–Sun., year-round. Web site: www.helicoptermuseum.org.

Brandywine Battlefield State Park, 1491 Baltimore Pike, Chadds Ford. Call 610-459-3342. Open for special events only.

Chester County Historical Society, 225 N. High Street, West Chester. Call 610-692-4800. Open Wed.–Sat., year-round. Web site: www.chesterco historical.org.

Longwood Gardens, 1001 Longwood Road, Kennett Square. Call 610-388-5200. Open daily, year-round. Web site: www.longwoodgardens.org.

The Mushroom Cap, 114 W. State Street, Kennett Square. Call 610-444-8484. Web site: www.themushroomcap.com.

Paoli Battlefield, Monument Avenue, Malvern. Call 866-650-7273. Web site: www.ushistory.org/paoli.

QVC Studio Park, 1200 Wilson Drive, West Chester. Call 800-600-9900. Open daily, year-round. Web site: www.qvctours.com.

Valley Forge National Historical Park, 1400 N. Outerline Drive, King of Prussia. Call 610-783-1099. Open daily, year-round. Web site: www.nps.gov/vafo.

Dining and Nightlife

Half Moon Restaurant and Saloon, 108 W. State Street, Kennett Square. Call 610-444-7232. Half Moon features an impressive lineup of wild game, including delicacies like alligator and antelope as well as more conventional New American choices made with local ingredients. Rooftop tables are the way to go when available. Open for lunch and dinner. Web site: www.halfmoonrestaurant.com.

Bike path and reconstructed shelters, Valley Forge

Northbrook Marketplace, 1805 Unionville Wawaset Road, West Chester. Call 610-793-1210. Web site: www.northbrookmarketplace.com.

Spence Café, 29–31 E. Gay Street, West Chester. Call 610-738-8844. A West Chester institution known for its seafood and live music late night. Open for lunch weekdays, dinner, and Sun. brunch. Web site: www.spence caferestaurant.com.

Talula's Table, 102 W. State Street, Kennett Square. Call 610-444-8255. It's close to impossible to get a dinner reservation at Talula's lone table (call at 7 AM a full year in advance), but you can still stop by during the day to pick up high-quality foods and prepared lunches from the market. Web site: www.talulastable.com.

Other Contacts

Chester County Conference & Visitors Bureau, 17 Wilmont Mews, Suite 400, West Chester. Call 610-719-1730. Web site: www.brandywine valley.com.

Bibliography

Bodnar, John. *Anthracite People: Families, Unions and Work, 1900–1940.* Harrisburg, PA: Pennsylvania Historical and Museum Commission, 1983.

Butko, Brian, and Kevin Patrick. *Diners of Pennsylvania.* Mechanicsburg, PA: Stackpole Books, 1999.

Cannadine, David. *Mellon: An American Life.* New York, NY: Random House, Inc., 2006.

Garrison, Webb. *A Treasury of Pennsylvania Tales.* Nashville, TN: Rutledge Hill Press, 1996.

Hunsinger, Louis, Jr., and Robin Van Auken. *Williamsport: Boomtown on the Susquehanna.* Charleston, SC: Arcadia Publishing, 2003.

Krass, Peter. *Carnegie.* Hoboken, NJ: John Wiley & Sons, Inc., 2002.

McGuire, Thomas J. *Battle of Paoli.* Mechanicsburg, PA: Stackpole Books, 2000.

McIlnay, Dennis P. *The Horseshoe Curve: Sabotage and Subversion in the Railroad City.* Hollidaysburg, PA: Seven Oaks Press, 2007.

————. *Juniata, River of Sorrows.* Hollidaysburg, PA: Seven Oaks Press, 2008.

Mitchell, Jeff. *Hiking the Allegheny National Forest.* Mechanicsburg, PA: Stackpole Books, 2007.

Oxford University Press. *Pennsylvania: A Guide to the Keystone State.* American Guide Series. New York, NY: Oxford University Press, 1940.

Palmer, Tim. *Rivers of Pennsylvania.* University Park, PA: Keystone Books, 1980.

Pippin, Bill. *Wood Hick, Pigs-Ear and Murphy.* 2nd ed. State College, PA: Jostens Printing and Pub, 1989.

Schafer, Mike, and Brian Solomon. *Pennsylvania Railroad.* Minneapolis, MN: Voyageur Press, 2009.

Speakman, Joseph M. *At Work in Penn's Woods: The Civilian Conservation Corps in Pennsylvania.* University Park, PA: The Pennsylvania State Press, 2006.

Squeri, Lawrence Louis. *Better in the Poconos.* University Park, PA: Keystone Books, 2002.

Stake, Virginia Ott. *John Brown in Chambersburg.* Chambersburg, PA: The Craft Press, 1977.

Tassin, Susan Hutchinson. *Pennsylvania Ghost Towns: Uncovering the Hidden Past.* Mechanicsburg, PA: Stackpole Books, 2007.

Treese, Lorett. *Railroads of Pennsylvania: Fragments of the Past in the Keystone Landscape.* Mechanicsburg, PA: Stackpole Books, 2003.

Wessman, Alice L. *A History of Elk County, Pennsylvania.* Ridgeway, PA: Elk County Historical Society, 1981.

Williams, Oliver P. *County Courthouses of Pennsylvania.* Mechanicsburg, PA: Stackpole Books, 2001.